The Revolutionized Church of the 21st Century

Russell Burrill

North American Division Evangelism Institute

HART RESEARCH CENTER
FALLBROOK, CALIFORNIA

Edited by Ken McFarland
Page composition by Page One Communications
Cover art direction and design by Ed Guthero
Illustrations by Sue Rother
Cloud pattern by Lars Justinen
Type set in 11.5/13 ITC Garamond Book

ISBN: 1-878046-45-4

Contents

About the Author

Russell Burrill, D. Min., is the Director of the North American Division Evangelism Institute in Berrien Springs, Michigan. He has served not only as a pastor and evangelist in many parts of the United States, but is also in great demand as a speaker and trainer.

In addition to presenting seminars on Bible prophecy to thousands across the United States and Canada and in overseas countries, Russell is at the forefront of today's renewed emphasis in the church on small-group fellowships, spiritual-gift-based church ministry, and lay evangelism.

This volume is the third in a trilogy of books dealing with revolutionary ideas on "reinventing" the church after New Testament and early Adventist patterns and practice.

Foreword

In the winter of 1988 I sat, awestruck, among a throng of worshipers that had crowded into the fifth of seven services at Paul Cho's Full Gospel Church on Oida Island in Seoul, Korea. Twenty thousand fervent attendees lifted up their voices in individual prayers. While I recognized unique differences between this megachurch and my own, it did not stop me from a kind of spiritual remorse brought on by the thought that my church in North America was not growing and experiencing kingdom building as was the one I was visiting.

A number of sources suggest that Paul Cho had access to the books *Evangelism* and *Gospel Workers* when he formulated the concepts for developing the largest church on the planet—boasting over 750,000 members and 50,000 small group leaders who meet every Wednesday night for instruction and empowerment. Cho claims "his church doesn't have a back door" where members slip away from fellowship. He can have this confidence, because the church is structured for member ministry in the small group setting. Members are discipled into more than 50,000 small groups, called cells. The DNA of these cells contains all of the ingredients of the full-blown church, including an equipping track that empowers and trains members to win someone for Christ from their circle of friends or acquaintances within three to nine months after they have joined the cell.

The cells are mandated to divide after they reach fifteen individuals, with the two new cells multiplying and dividing in turn. Thus, every convert has a shepherd, a support group, and a ministry with fruit.

At first consideration, we often rationalize that mega-churches such as Cho's do not have the doctrinal challenges we face when attempting to reach potential converts. Thus, we conjecture, "it is easy for them to grow."

However, in a number of these churches, the demands for members to commit to ministry is much more intentional than our own. The question comes: "Is it easier to commit to doctrines and lifestyle—or to a lifelong commitment to ministry and soul winning within a relational small group church?" At least one megachurch requires its members to be involved in ministry in order to be in good and regular standing. Membership is reviewed annually to determine if the member is carrying out the gospel commission. The assumption is that at conversion, members are endowed with spiritual gifts that the Holy Spirit gives them to edify the church. If a member is not engaged in ministry, the conclusion is that they have not responded to the Holy Spirit's benevolence. They have no evidence of joining the body of Christ, if no gift is manifested. This book challenges the membership of the Seventh-day Adventist Church to return to the relational church of the New Testament and early Adventism, with its "social meeting."

Russell Burrill, in *The Revolutionized Church of the 21st Century*, joins the ranks of the bold pioneers whose messages anchored the remnant church and set it on a course to win the world. He not only challenges the membership to discipleship, but to the *koinonia* (communion) found in the relational model of the New Testament Church, where the Christian community of small groups nurtured and evangelized without depending on a paid clergy. "They had all things common . . . And none lacked . . . and they added to the church daily such as should be saved" (Acts 2:44, 47).

While tens of thousands of hours and nearly two decades have consumed church leaders with the notion that the upper tiers of the Church (conference, union, division, and General Conference) needed reorganization, precious little has been done to reengineer the local church, where the DNA of Kingdom growth is housed. Fortunately, this book is a "back-to-the-future" road map that has no need to mirror corporate America's right-sizing experiments. The author can rely on the most successful model known to mankind—the New Testament diaspora—which seeded the earth with small relational groups that nurtured its members and evangelized the world, one family circle at a time. Russell Burrill has literally traced this revolutionary model of local church structure from its source—the Truine God. Like a skilled tailor, he further has drawn together biblical and historical patterns connected and verified by the incontrovertible thread of the Spirit of Prophecy.

Of great interest is the way the author has enunciated the role of the pastor as a trainer and equipper who empowers lay people to care for themselves in small groups, while the pastor plants new churches and expands the work of God in unentered areas. The pastor's role is not just to sermonize but to equip members. This book not only has the potential for reengineering the local church but also for "reinventing" the pastor. Again, the author has a marvelous safety net which shelters these concepts from just another visionary speculation. It is based firmly on Scripture and corroborated in the Spirit of Prophecy writings in describing what the role and function of the pastor should be. It is very different from what we witness today in our churches.

So how did we get so far off in our ecclesiology? The author does a very credible job of tracing many of our practices back to religious paradigms introduced in the fourth century when Emporer Constantine the Great joined the Christian faith and brought with him the Roman ecclesiastical systems. One such system was an institutionalized church that dismantled the small-group relational communities which had flourished for three hundred years since the days of the apostles. Another was the dominance of the clergy class, which denied the universal priesthood of the believers—the idea that every member was a minister. This created a spectator class who were not empowered to minister or even to read the Scriptures. That was reserved for the clergy. A byproduct of this today is the cry among many members that the pastor is "not feeding me." Also seen is the 80/20 syndrome, which church growth watchers declare as one of the great maladies afflicting Christianity—a dependent laity in which 80 percent of the members wait for the 20 percent of professional and paid clergy to serve them.

Burrill is not reticent to remind the readers of this volume that the heresies of Mystery Babylon relate to structure and practice as well as to doctrine. The pristine doctrine that does not have the proper structural vehicle to carry it to the world stymies God's work as surely as a false doctrine that spreads.

The appeal to "come out of Babylon" is made in this book, not as a call to exit from doctrinal heresies, but in reference to the local church structure which neutered the small-group relational community and took on the institutional program based design bequeathed to all of Christendom by the Roman Church.

If the phenomenon of a newly emerging cell church movement is a "Second Reformation," as William Beckham asserts in his book, *The Second Reformation,* then the rise of the small relational group structure is for Adventism the "Third Reformation"—the first in 1516, the second in 1844, and the third today. Nowhere is this more evident than in the book you are reading now. Russell Burrill does an excellent job of bridging the history from the Adventist roots in Methodism to the early ecclesiology which birthed the Adventist version of John Wesley's small companies and Sunday school classes. Unlike Jonathan Edwards and George Whitfield, both powerful eighteenth-century revivalists, John Wesley laid out an organizational method of small relational groups that has become one of our most valuable legacies and practices up to the death of Ellen White. For the first time in revolutionay church, this connectivity is uncovered in the context of today's local church structure.

The author introduces to his readers the "social meetings" so often referred to by Ellen White. In the following chapters you will learn why these meetings were considered more important than the so called Divine Worship preaching hour. It will be interesting to note how passionate Ellen White was about this small group relational meeting called the "social meeting." She spoke of it taking place in different parts of the world field, at General Conference sessions, and at our hospitals. She insisted that every member should attend this function. No preaching service seemed to be complete unless this "social meeting" followed it. Where would this gathering fit in today's church? Read on.

I attended a strategic planning session where the noted Leland Kaiser, a leading futurist who happens to be an Adventist, challenged the group to reverse their assumptions so they could see new ways of looking at the future. He said, "You cannot be a visionary unless you reverse your assumptions." Here are some examples of reversing assumptions—for instance, people come to church. Reversed—the church goes to the people. Here's another—enlarge the church. Reversed—shrink the church. Believe it or not, this book is about reversing the assumption of enlarging the church. It is about shrinking the church for optimum growth. This does not mean that we cut down the membership. It means that we shrink the sum of its parts to the least common denominator—small relational groups.

That is the way nature operates. It delegates functions down to the closest functioning part. So a paper cut is handled by the cells at the point of the injury—not by the brain. It may sound like an oxymoron to shrink the church for it to grow, but in fact, it is the formula of the New Testament strategy. When the Roman system enlarged the church from small relational groups, turning it into a cathedral full of people dependent on a few elite clerics, the church lost its fire, and the gradual chill of Laodecea began to set in. Russell Burrill, in a sense, is suggesting that we reverse our assumptions by shrinking the church to small relational groups that carry the DNA of the mission of Christ, or at least reintroduce the relational aspects of New Testament life back into today's church. While the ideal structure modeled after the early church is set forth in this volume, the author offers options that take into account the varied levels of readiness for innovation, even when concepts are substantiated in the Bible and Spirit of Prophecy. This book is sensitive to this and yet, for balance's sake, the author acknowledges the resistance that can come when a new paradigm is interjected.

This book will raise many queries. However, few will be able to challenge its biblical, historical, and Spirit of Prophecy moorings. It is a revolutionary affront to the American Individualism which recoils from relational paradigms. Consequently, it will disturb the culture of Western Society. Those who read these pages and are able to implement its concepts will be marching in step with the greatest religious renaissance of all times. It has striking parallels to the discovery the Japanese made when Total Quality Management concepts were introduced to them by an American named Edward Deming. Corporate America rejected Deming's ideas, so he took them to the Japanese. The Japanese accepted and incorporated the concepts, along with what they called the Quality Circle—a small relational self-management group formed to add value to the products manufactured. Together this small group would add value to the products and share ideas to improve them over the preceding day. This concept led to zero defects and to a country the size of the state of Montana capturing the major world markets from the U.S. and other Western nations.

The book entitled *The Art of Japanese Management* asserts that the influence of the Roman Church on the governance structures of Western Society allowed Japan, which was not under its influence, to be more receptive to innovative approaches. They were able to think outside the box—to reverse their assumptions and take the lead in World War III—the economic war.

The *Revolutionized Church of the 21st Century* is about breaking out of the paradigm prisons in which Rome has incarcerated all of Western Society, not only affecting our economic productivity but shackling us to a hierarchical pyramid structure that leaves no room for relational self-management small groups. It has frozen us in "American Individualism"—a crypt that resists the notion of anything that resembles what we see in the first ten chapters of the book of Acts. This individualism leads to judgmentalism, which hatches separatism, which is akin to tribalism, nationalism, and racism.

If as you read these pages, you see something that seems to be upside down to you, remember that Galileo stood the universe on its head—and he was right. Jesus was the greatest of all upside down thinkers. "When you go out take no gold, script or purse, no change of cloak, abide with those that receive you. . . Take no thought of what you will say when they pull you before the court . . . he that loseth his life for my sake shall find it."

—Aldwin Humphries

1

Back to Our Roots, Forward to the Future

Imagine the Seventh-day Adventist Church in the year 2010, if Christ does not come before then. What will it look like? Will it be a church animated and vitalized by the Holy Spirit, faithfully fulfilling the mission of Christ? How will it "do church?" A Holy Spirit–energized church will be faithful to our Adventist heritage and beliefs, but it also will be in tune with the world it is trying to reach. Therefore, it may do things differently than many Adventist churches today, but it will still be faithful to our message and mission.

Seventh-day Adventism was born as a biblical movement. Our heritage is deeply rooted in Scripture. Our church grows rapidly around the world because of its strong emphasis on biblical teachings. Early Adventism built its faith and teachings squarely on Scripture. The early pioneers were concerned about building a church that was biblical in practice, as well. In other words, they sought not only to construct a church based on correct teachings but also one in harmony with the practice and organization of the New Testament Church.

Interestingly, early Adventists did not seek simply to copy the New Testament church but consciously tried to build a church around the principles laid down in the New Testament for how the church lived. Modern Adventism has attempted to remain faithful to our biblical heritage on the teachings of the church, but has allowed unbiblical practices to creep into our churches concerning how we "do church." In a desire to not be seen as different from other Protestant churches, we have simply copied their systems and incorporated them into our church. As a result, we now have all the same problems most main-line churches have—attendance is about half the membership, giving levels are on the decline, people operate at a low commitment level, and pastors are happy if the members simply show up on Sabbath morning.

It is time to take a fresh look at how we "do church" in Adventism. Many local churches stand in desperate need of rejuvenation. As a result, we listen to the latest fad and try it out in the church. Some fads are good—some are miserable failures. Rather than simply accepting the latest ideas to hit the circuit, it would be far better for us to examine the Scriptures, our Adventist heritage, and the writings of Ellen White to discover God's plan for how we should "do church."

It will be the function of this book to examine a biblical view for the way God intends the church to operate and to offer suggestions for creating a revolutionized church that is faithful not only to the teachings of Scripture but also to the principles on which the practice of the church is built. The two previous books in this series, *Revolution in the Church* and *Radical Disciples for Revolutionary Churches*, have laid the foundation for the picture we will draw in this book: a church designed to operate on the New Testament basis of doing church in the twenty-first century. That's why we must go back to our roots if we are to move forward to the future.

Small Group Phenomenon

Over the last several years, the small group phenomenon has mushroomed across North America and around the world. Both within the Adventist church and in other denominations, a movement has taken place that is truly transforming the church and the world. Many Adventist congregations have begun the process of "reinventing" their churches around small groups. A national prayer and small group conference meets at least once a year and many regional conventions are being held on a regular basis. Truly there is much interest in small groups within the Adventist church today.

Yet amazingly, little consideration has been paid to an Adventist theological or historical understanding of small groups. In spite of the plethora of small group books within and without the Adventist church, little has been written on the biblical basis for small group ministry. Plenty of "how to" books are available. All the mechanics of running successful small groups and training good small group leaders are available at any Adventist Book Center or other Christian retailer.

The purpose of this book is not to duplicate the "how to's." The reader is advised to consult the many books and manuals already prepared in that area. Instead, the purpose of this work is to explore a biblical rationale for small group community. We Adventists profess to be a biblical people, to base all that we believe and practice solely on Scripture. On that basis it is disappointing that we have entered a practics area devoid of major theological consideration. Have we simply jumped onto a popular bandwagon, or is the small group movement deeply rooted in the way Christ intended His church to operate?

In addition to the biblical perspective, we Adventists also have the advantage of examining our historical roots to discover if this is an area of church life that our pioneers, and especially Ellen White, emphasized at all. Therefore, we will thoroughly examine not only the biblical basis for small group ministry but also the historical beginning of Adventism as it relates to small groups as a way of "doing church." We will also examine the many statements of Ellen White dealing with small group ministry. We will then suggest steps Adventism needs to take in the area of small group ministry to bring us back to our biblical and historical roots. Hopefully, this study will give us a glimpse of the revolutionized church of the twenty-first century.

As we talk about Adventism in this book, the author is primarily referring to western Adventism, especially North American Adventism, rather than third world Adventism. In North America a few churches have broken through and created real "community" through small groups. However, the vast majority that have tried small groups have merely added small groups to an already overloaded local church program, with the result being that the small groups do not become a major way that we "do church" in North America. The ultimate end is that small groups function for awhile and then are dropped from the overloaded program, and we become further discouraged with trying anything new.

It is the contention of this writer that the essence of what small groups is all about is the heart of what church is all about: community. Small groups are not a panacea for all the ills of the church. Small groups will not save a dying church or rejuvenate a declining one. It is only the Holy Spirit operating within our churches who can bring real change. But small groups may be a major vehicle to facilitate the outpouring of the Holy Spirit. Only the presence of Jesus can transform people, and His presence is made manifest through the Holy Spirit, who facilitates the growth of individuals and the mission of the church through small group communities.

Rugged American individualism tends to cause Americans to think they can serve God apart from any attachment to a community of believers. How often the author has heard individuals in evangelistic meetings declare that they believe

God's message, but they do not wish to unite with the church. In fact, one researcher has claimed that fully 80 percent of American Christians believe they can be good Christians without being a part of the church.[1] Such a comment, it will be shown, would be absolutely foreign to the thinking of first-century Christians.

Could it be that involvement in a community of believers is what is desperately needed by most American Christians today? Rather than this being an option for Christians, the thesis of this book is that it is impossible to be a Christian and not be involved in community. Isolated Christians are not really biblical Christians, even though their names are on the books of our churches. Community is not gained by membership, but neither is it attained without membership. Caring communities where people truly minister to one another are the basis upon which all real mission can happen in Adventist churches at the beginning of the new millennium.

Modern Adventist churches have become so pastor dependent that without the pastor, no real ministry is possible in most churches. As a result, we have a burned-out, frustrated clergy, from whose ranks many excellent pastors are exiting year by year. The challenges of pastoring as we enter the twenty-first century are not going to be met by asking pastors to become better skilled in more areas. We don't need to add to their frustrations. We need to take away their frustration and release them for the ministry God has called them to do. Carl George, church growth consultant, has described the need of most Adventist churches well:

> Show me a pastor-centered large church, and we'll find a very tired staff of clergy. Show me a lay-empowered, simply organized large church, where the clergy are not completely exhausted because they're doing too much, and I will show you a church that will not stop growing because it will be able to take good care of people as God calls them to new life through it.[2]

Are small groups the answer? No, but they may be one of the means that can be used to revolutionize the church. The primary objective of small groups is to create a community that cares, as it reaches out to share Christ with those who do not know Him. One of the best ways to accomplish that, this author believes, is through the initiation of a small group ministry. The development of the caring community as the basis for the fulfillment of the mission of Christ will be explored through the rest of this book.

Over the pages that follow, we will examine a biblical foundation for small groups as seen from the Old Testament record, the ministry of Jesus, life in the New Testament church, and the kind of churches established by the apostle Paul. We will then examine our Methodist heritage, from which our pioneers borrowed much of the original way that they "did church." Examinations of early Adventist church life and the prophetic testimony of Ellen White will further help us understand God's plan for the Seventh-day Adventist Church to be a relational church. Finally, we will suggest a possible model for the revolutionized church of the twenty-first century-a model in harmony with our biblical, historical, and Spirit of Prophecy roots. Let's begin with Scripture.

Notes:

1. Gareth Icenogle, *The Church in Ministry Through Small Groups*, 1995.

2. Carl F. George, *The Coming Church Revolution* (Grand Rapids: Revell, 1995), 35.

2

The Beginning of Community

Human beings are basically communal. We were not made to live alone but to live in community with others. This need to live in community is God-created, inherent in our very being. Humanity likewise was created in the image of God, which would thereby indicate that the infinite God of the universe also lives in community. What does the Old Testament reveal about the God who lives in community and the beings He created to live in community with each other?

In the vastness of eternity, the God of the Bible has always existed. He is the One God, who created heaven and earth. Yet the "oneness" of our God is not expressed in "singleness" but in trinity. The biblical God is never presented in Scripture as a single entity but as a plurality that is "one." Adventists, along with most other Christians, have always spoken of God as "Trinity." The three members of the Godhead—Father, Son, and Holy Spirit—are three separate persons but one in character, unity, and purpose. We do not understand the oneness of God apart from the plurality of that oneness.

It is in this sense that the Godhead itself is a small group. In fact, observing and studying the Godhead and how it functions is the best guide one can have for understanding how a small group should operate. The Godhead is the perfect community and provides the guidelines for how true community is to be expressed. We Adventists have sensed that God has called us to help restore people to the image of God. If that truly is our mission, then we must recognize that God's image cannot be restored unless humankind is relationally restored to live in community with each other, just as do the Father, Son, and Holy Spirit. Inherent in the Adventist understanding of mission is a restoration of community. That should place small groups that restore community at the very center of Adventist mission.

The three members of the Trinity did not act alone in the creation of the earth. We have often described God the Father as the architect, Christ as the foreman, and the Holy Spirit as the worker. The three as a unit acted together in the creation of humankind and everything that is on this planet. From examining the workings of God in human history, it becomes clear that no member of the Trinity ever acts independently of the other two members. The uniqueness of the one God is seen in their perfect harmony as they work together. The Godhead is indeed the perfect small group that all small groups should emulate.

The essence of God is community. God Himself does not exist apart from community. At God's very heart and center is the whole idea of community. One cannot truly understand God apart from His existence in community. And as God does not exist alone, neither can His people. That's why God is calling for small groups where people live in community with each other. In a world destroyed by broken communities, God is seeking to restore in converted humanity a demonstration of what genuine community is all about, because genuine community is a reflection of the God who lives in community. It is impossible to restore humanity to the image of God without a restoration of community.

Creation and Community

The first activity of the God of community upon planet earth was the creation, and especially the creation of humankind on the sixth day:

> Then God said, "Let Us make man in Our image, according to Our likeness, and let them rule over the fish of the sea and over the birds of the sky and over the cattle and over all the earth, and over every creeping thing that creeps on the earth."
>
> And God created man in His own image, in the image of God He created him, male and female He created them.[1]

Humankind is expressly said to be created in the image of the triune God. Humankind has been created to live in community, just as God exists in community. The use of the plural, "our," to describe the image of God points to the fact that the image of God is community. The God who exists in community has created beings who are to exist in the same kind of oneness in community.

On the sixth day God grew His small group by creating a new pair who would exist not only in community with each other, but in community with God. Thus, God's small group had grown to five: Adam, Eve, and the Triune God. As soon as Adam was created, God had already anticipated his "aloneness" and created a "helpmate" for him.

> Then the Lord God said, "It is not good for the man to be alone, I will make him a helper suitable for him."[2]

"It is not good for man to be alone." Human beings were not created to live by themselves. They were created to live in community with each other and with God. This is the essence of true community—human beings living together in community with each other and with God. A leading characteristic of sin is the attempt to live apart from community, to live in isolation from others. Human beings, however, are not complete apart from fellowship with others. The beauty of Eden is seen in the perfect community that existed with God and humankind. Man is not complete without Woman, for the totality of the two equals the image of God. Male or female alone is not God's image, for God is triune and humankind is a minimum of two people living in community with each other. There is no true humanity apart from community as a reflection of the divine image.

To this perfect community that God had created, He gave one clear command: "Be fruitful and multiply, and fill the earth" (Genesis 1:28, NASB). In this first "cell" that God had created at the very beginning of human history, God placed a genetic code of reproduction. The "cell" existed for the sake of reproduction. Genuine community exists to multiply itself. Any community not engaged in multiplying itself is destructive community. Healthy community reproduces itself. That is part of our genetic code issuing from the perfect paradise of Eden. Inherent in any understanding of small "cell" groups is this most basic of functions: healthy cell groups will be multiplying themselves, just as God commanded the first "cell" that He created to multiply and fill the earth.

If it is God's purpose, as Adventists so often propose, to create a people who reflect the image of God to the world, then it would seem that at the heart of Adventism must be the desire to restore broken communities into communities that reflect the divine image. Therefore the Adventist church must be in the forefront of any movement that seeks to restore broken communities to the image of God. Not only must Adventists be creating these communities, we also must be engaged in multiplying healthy communities.

Within Adventism is a strong, independent spirit. Could it be that Adventism, birthed in America, has unwittingly accepted the rugged individualism of America as gospel? Have we, who talk so much about creation, failed to see the initial purpose of God in the creation of our first parents—to live in community with each other and with God? Why do we as Adventists strive against each other to create our own success, rather than community success? As Judy Gorman has aptly observed:

> The self-sufficiency and personal independence that characterize our present evaluation of success is totally foreign to the Godhead who exist in interdependent community.[3]

If we are going to reflect the divine image in our church, it is imperative that we develop a church with respect for community and a willingness to live in subjection to each other in such a community, as that community is in subjection to the Godhead. We must banish the rewards of individual accomplishment and uphold the ideal of group accomplishment. God intends that we live in interdependence with each other rather than in competition with each other. This concept of interdependence in community is rooted in the triune God and in the very creation that He made in "Our" (plural) image. God does not create one-person societies, He only creates community. The God who lives in a group creates a group.

The practical ramification of seeing God as the Creator of community is to see our absolute need to live in community with other Christians. In this sense, it is impossible to be a Christian and live in isolation, for to do so is to live apart from the image of God and the purpose of God for humankind.

How often we have heard an individual declare that he or she can be just as good a Christian apart from the church. Yet understanding the function of community as the image of God renders such a statement anathema. There is no Christianity apart from community. As much as people may try, they can never be restored to the image of God apart from involvement in a community. This involvement in community is not simply being a member of the church or even attending church. Involvement in community means to live in mutual dependency on other Christians. Gorman has insightfully declared:

> Biblically . . . we need community to fulfill our pull in the direction of reflecting the image of God. This awareness of and interdependency with others is part of our creation format. We will never be whole apart from giving ourselves away to others and receiving from them their uniqueness. For believers, to be in Christ is to be in relationship with others in His body.[4]

The Purpose of Biblical Community

God indeed has created humanity to live in community, just as the Trinity lives in community. What then is the purpose of this community that God has established? That purpose can be understood only in the light of Eden. We have already noticed one inherent purpose in the creation of this first community: reproduction. The Edenic scene now pictures a second function of true biblical community.

Humankind had been created by God on the sixth day. As the sun sank in the west on that first Friday evening, God announced the beginning of His Sabbath, the seventh day. At that time God set aside the seventh day as a sacred respite time for humans to spend with Him and with each other. We Adventists have spent much time talking about the "seventh dayness" of the Sabbath, and rightly so, but hopefully in the process of emphasizing the day we have not forgotten the purpose of that day.

In the hectic schedule of modern life, we have tended to emphasize the value of Sabbath rest, as a respite from the mayhem of modern living. As a result, we have talked much about "resting" on the Sabbath. Yet the original function of the Sabbath was not rest, and that should not be the main focus today. Adam and Eve had no need of rest. They had done no work. Their first day on the planet was the Sabbath. They were asked to cease from their work, not for the sake of human rest, but for the purpose of entering into relationship with the infinite God of the universe.

In giving the Sabbath as a gift to humankind, God refers to it as "My" Sabbath. It is not a Sabbath to celebrate humankind's rest. It is a celebration of God's rest. Humankind are invited to enter into God's rest by ceasing from their own works, as God did from His on the seventh day (Hebrews 4:10). Why does God ask humans to enter into His Sabbath rest? In order that they might spend time developing community with Him and with one another. Adam and Eve needed to get acquainted with the God who had made them. Thus God invited them to spend their first twenty-four hours in community with Him.

Our God is a God of relationships. He is a God of community. It is imperative for us as Adventists, with our Sabbath emphasis, to talk about the function of the Sabbath as a time for humans and God to enter into relationship with one another. This is why our Sabbath message is so necessary for today's world—not just that the hectic pace of society demands a day of rest, but that we must have a special day to emphasize community. On Sabbath God intends for us to come apart from all the broken communities that we have to function in throughout the week in order that we might participate in a community that is being renewed through a relationship with God. Human tragedy occurs, many times, because we fail to see real community being developed in our churches on Sabbath. Many times we discover people "keeping" the seventh day, but totally divorced from building a relationship with God and with other Christians. Unless one is building a relationship in community, one is a Sabbath breaker.

To keep the Sabbath alone is thus in reality not keeping the Sabbath at all, for the purpose of the Sabbath is to develop a relationship with God in the setting of community with other Christians.

The God of relationships has created humankind not only to live in community with each other but also to live in community with God. In addition, He has provided a special time, set aside from Eden, for the human race to leave the brokenness and destruction of human works communities and to enter the joy of Sabbath rest, taking time to develop the vertical relationship with God in community and horizontally with humankind. Only thus can the divine image be restored. Adventists, of all Christians, should be preaching and demonstrating the results of living in community on the seventh day.

Such communities are not developed simply by being in a large group in church on Sabbath morning, listening to a preacher expound the Word as worshipers examine the back of each others' heads. That is the antithesis of real community. Such an understanding of God and humans in community on Sabbath may indicate that we must discover a new way of "doing church" that is far different from the Middle Ages nonparticipatory model currently in use. Since Sabbath morning worship is the primary activity for most Adventists today, it may mean creating an entirely new model of church on Sabbath morning. We will explore such a model later in this book. Whatever we do on Sabbath must be for the purpose of building a relationship with God in community with each other. All activities must be examined in light of this function. So let us examine what we do on Sabbath morning and ask ourselves the question: Does this activity build community? It doesn't mean these noncommunity-building activities are wrong. However, if only noncommunity-building activities are done, then we have missed the essence of what it means to be church—to live in community.

The apostle John succinctly states this to be the basic purpose for the church gathered:

> What was from the beginning, what we have heard, what we have seen with our eyes, what we beheld and our hands handled, concerning the Word of Life—and the life was manifested, and we have seen and bear witness and proclaim to you the eternal life, which was with the Father and was

manifested to us-what we have seen and heard we proclaim to you also, that you also may have fellowship with us, and indeed our fellowship is with the Father, and with His Son Jesus Christ.[5]

Even the apostle John recognizes that the innate function of the preaching of the Word is to create communities that are both vertical and horizontal; fellowship with God and fellowship with one another. The Word is not preached for the sake of securing intellectual assent to certain dogmas. The Word is preached so that community (fellowship) can be restored, both to God and to humankind. This is the essence of the creation story and is the essence of the mission of Christ, according to the apostle John. There can be no church if community is not created.

Notes:

1. Gen. 1:26, 27, *New American Standard Bible* (NASB).

2. Gen. 2:18, NASB.

3. Judy Gorman, *Community That is Christian: A Handbook on Small Groups* (Wheaton, IL: Victor Books, 1993) 28.

4. Gorman, 107.

5. 1 John 1:1-3, NASB.

3

God's Attempts At Restoring Community

Humankind came forth from the hand of God a perfect creation, made in the image of God. Having been made in that image entailed the human race living in community with each other and with the Trinity, as the Trinity lived in community. Eden existed only as Adam and Eve continued to live in true community with the Godhead. As soon as community with the Godhead was broken, humankind entered a world of broken community. This break was twofold: humans no longer lived in community with God or with each other. The biblical story is the account of God's attempts to restore the broken community which sin had created.

Genesis 3 tells the sad story of the loss of that innocent community. As soon as Eve had partaken of the forbidden fruit, she quickly convinced her husband to join her in sin. Something in the carnal heart causes people to feel better if they are not alone in wrongdoing. They feel self-justified if others are involved.

The state of innocence depicted by Adam and Eve's nakedness revealed that they were totally open to each other and to God—the ideal of full community. They enjoyed complete transparency with each other. No sooner had our first parents sinned than they noticed that they were naked and sought to hide from God (Genesis 3:6, 7). Here is revealed the brokenness of community that sin has created. Open communities are rare as human beings attempt to hide their true selves from each other and from God. The mission of Christ is to restore what was broken and to create new, open communities (Luke 4:18). Churches engaged in the mission of Christ will be attempting to create open communities reflective of our Edenic origins.

No one told Adam and Eve that they were naked. They passed judgment on themselves and on God, whom they thought would no longer be interested in a relationship with them. A knowledge of good and evil leads to judgmentalism. It is this spirit which has destroyed community throughout human history and is the largest destroyer of community even in this age. People in sin always try to pass judgment on others in an attempt to avoid being judged wrong themselves. Such judgmentalism is seen in the office when the boss tries to blame a subordinate for the mistake he has made. It is seen in the home when the husband attempts to blame the wife for not disciplining the children. It is seen in the church when the pastor attempts to blame the church for his failures, the implication being that if he had a better church he could do a better job. All of this judgmentalism is destructive to the kind of community God wishes to create.

Jesus came to reconcile humankind. How did He do it? By taking judgment on Himself and not turning it back. He became sin and received in His person God's judgment on sin. He did not attempt to place judgment on humankind, for He was restoring lost community, and that can only be done by declining to pass judgment on those who give it. Leaders who can take judgment and not turn it back are redeeming leaders. These are the kind of people who are needed as small group leaders today. Leaders who return judgment will produce dysfunctional groups, whereas leaders who demonstrate acceptance and love will create redeeming groups. Community is restored when judgment is received but not returned; community is lost when people pass judgment on themselves and on the community. Judgmentalism is the greatest curse to true community.

What was lost in Eden was true community, a place where humankind can know God and each other through deep personal relationships. God created humankind to live with each other in mutual dependence. Sin causes people to desire to live independently from one another. The destructiveness of our society today is seen in the millions of people both inside and outside the church who are attempting to live independently, when they have been created to live in dependence.

As a result of the independent spirit which controls humanity in this age, most people continually pass judgment on each other. For this reason, it is necessary that people today be in redeeming groups, which require a small group leader who does not pass judgment on the group but models the redemptive community Jesus sought to establish. One of the functions of small groups is to provide a safe place where humanity can be healed of its brokenness. Redeeming groups of people who refuse to pass judgment on each other can, through the power of the Holy Spirit, actually reverse the fall. People who seek to live independently of others and fail to be part of a redeeming group cannot be healed of their brokenness.

The Formation of Destructive Communities

Genesis 4 reveals the next step in the downward spiral of the loss of community. Here the children of Adam and Eve pass judgment on each other and commit murder. Murder is the ultimate result of hiding from God and from each other and judging one another. That is why Jesus declared that he who is angry with his brother has committed murder (Matt.

5:21, 22). If we wish to stop the deluge of murder in our society, we need to teach people to stop hiding from each other and from God. Most murders occur within families. This is due to families being dysfunctional communities where individualism prevails. Not only can the restoration of true community prevent murder in the family and society, but the restoration of true community in the church can prevent the "murdering" that is going on because of people passing judgment on each other. As the dysfunction of the family has been transferred to the church, many churches have become dysfunctional communities. Failure to deal with the restoration of true community hinders the church from playing in the world the redemptive role that God desires.

Dysfunctional churches are created whenever members live independently from each other instead of maintaining the mutual dependence advocated by the Edenic ideal. In dysfunctional churches, when a member sins the church becomes more concerned about passing judgment on the sin than in saving and helping the sinner. Such churches are quick to take ecclesiastical action to discipline, but rarely work to restore the one who has fallen. In a dysfunctional church, when a pastor has a moral fall the church is quick to take action to remove the pastor from his position, and rightly so; however, that is the end of the matter. The church has acted, and the pastor/sinner is left to fend for himself.

In a healthy church, action will be taken, but the wounded sinner will not be left alone; the church will seek to restore the pastor. In fact, healthy churches are more eager to help restore than to pass judgment. They have been able to separate the sin from the sinner. Likewise, in healthy churches a member who slips and smokes does not remain away from the church for fear of condemnation. Instead, this individual feels comfortable coming to the church, knowing that the church will not condemn but will provide the help needed for restoration. The healthy redemptive community is the ideal that bears witness to the world that the church really knows Jesus. Sinners loved Jesus, and sinners will love the church that reflects Jesus' method of dealing with sinners.

A prime example of this is the Bible story of the woman caught in adultery. Rather than place judgment on the woman, Jesus releases the woman and tells her, "Go, and sin no more" (John 8:11). Immediately following this story, John places the account of Jesus talking to the Pharisees about judging. Notice what Jesus declares: "You people judge according to the flesh; I am not judging anyone."[1] This behavior is opposite that of people in the dysfunctional community, who are always passing judgment on each other. God has called the church to be a community that follows Jesus by accepting, affirming, and loving one another, not judging. The church ought to be known in the community as a "safe" place, where people can be themselves and know that they will still be accepted. That is the evidence that the church is the redemptive community God wants it to be.

Cain and Abel both brought offerings before God. While God had specified a blood offering, Cain brought instead the fruit of the ground. Abel had brought a blood offering. Abel's offering was accepted, while Cain's was rejected. Why? Abel cared for sheep. It was easy for him to bring an offering of the flock, but Cain tilled the ground. In order to bring a blood offering, he would have had to depend on his brother. That he refused to do. The sin of Cain was individualism a failure to depend on community. The result was immediate self-justification, anger, and, ultimately, murder.

Yet God did not return judgment on Cain. The heart of the seeking God of Scripture is seen in His attempt to reach Cain. God wanted above everything else to have a relationship with Cain, as He had with Abel. God is the great restorer of broken relationships and community. So instead of passing judgment on Cain, He allowed him to wander across the face of the earth, hoping that someday he would return to God.

The issue in the story of Cain and Abel is the need of community. As soon as Cain had killed his brother, God called to him and asked where his brother was. Cain's response: "I do not know. Am I my brother's keeper?"[2] reveals the truth that we need to learn from this story. God wants us to understand that we are indeed our brother's keeper. The world today follows Cain's example and does not care about being their brother's keeper. Cain's response indicates his failure to understand God's plan for people to be in community with one another. He rejects community and embraces individualism.

After wandering the face of the earth, Cain eventually settled in Nod, married, and had a son, Enoch. At this juncture, Scripture declares that Cain built a city,[3] which he named after his son. When people build cities for themselves, they are departing from genuine community. Out of Cain's rebellion, he built a city. Cities arose out of broken communities. It is not God's plan for humanity to live in cities. The closer people live together, as they do in cities, the less they know one another and the less community is present. The ultimate sign of the city is the rebellion that occurred at the tower of Babel. At this time, God divided humanity so that they scattered into smaller groups across the earth.

The children of Cain build cities. Cities originate as people rebel from God and the community He wishes to establish among His children. Broken relationships do not build community—they build cities where people are distant from one another. A city as defined here is not the literal city, although it can include that. Rather, a city is defined as any place where people are living close together but not in community. Many "country" churches in this sense are cities, fortresses where people hide from each other rather than live in dependence upon each other.

Today the brokenness of humanity is revealed in our great cities. We have cities, but we do not have community. Cities are community killers. It is the responsibility of churches, even those literally located in cities, to seek to build community in these cities. Yet instead of building community, we see churches building great empires to themselves. God is not impressed with the great structures we create or the mammoth institutions we build. His plan does not call for large organizations but for community. Large and even small churches can be like cities. People can be lost in the congregation, and even though they attend every Sabbath, they fail to discover community.

Unless a church develops small relational groups where people can find community, it is still partaking of the spirit of Cain in building a city rather than seeking to help people find real community. Cities are pseudo-communities. Millions of people are controlled by people in power. When this happens, there is no community, either in the world or in the church. The gathering of people into smaller groups results in the building of community. Churches that exist in the city, then, must concentrate on building community in the city rather than attempting to accumulate power.

However, we need to realize that a city mentality can exist even in the country, and destructive community can exist in small groups. What we are talking about here is not a particular place (city or country), but an attitude. Whenever and wherever people are attempting to exercise power over others, the result is a city. Whenever and wherever people are isolated from each other and real community does not exist, the result is a city. God's plan for His people is the restoration of community, a place where people can be open and vulnerable to each other, where no one needs to hide. As Gareth Icenogle has said:

> Genesis 1-11 is about a theology of community in paradox and appears as a countermovement with the establishment of cities and civilization. Broken humanity builds cities. Covenant humanity builds covenant family communities.[4]

In the midst of our lonely, crowded cities today, humanity desperately longs for community. When they fail to find it in the church, they seek to discover it elsewhere. The result is seen in many dysfunctional groups of people. While longing for genuine community, people end up in pseudo communities. Perhaps the best counterfeit to the community of the church is the bar:

> The neighborhood bar is possibly the best counterfeit there is to the fellowship Christ wants to give His church. It's an imitation, dispensing liquor instead of grace, escape rather than reality, but it is a permissive, accepting, and inclusive fellowship. It is unshockable. It is democratic. You can tell people secrets and they usually don't tell others or even want to. The bar flourishes not because people are alcoholics, but because God has put into the human heart the desire to know and be known, to love and be loved. (Swindoll, 128)[5]

Humankind desperately needs community today. People need a place where they can be loved and cared for, where they can be open and vulnerable and not be judged. This is the kind of community that Scripture holds out from its very inception. It is time for the church of Jesus Christ to return to building community rather than reflecting the brokenness of the communities all around us.

The small group will not necessarily solve the problem of the lack of community in churches, but it does provide a vehicle where community is more apt to occur than in the loneliness found in the crowds of most of our churches. God wants us to really know each other, to be accountable to each other, to minister to each other, and to truly enter into community with each other.

Deliverance From Egypt

As God prepared to call into existence His chosen people, Israel, He first needed to find a leader who could model genuine community. That leader was Moses. Yet Moses was not by nature God's kind of community builder. He had been educated in all the wisdom of Egypt. His education had actually prepared him for leadership in a dysfunctional way.

Egypt's leadership style is best symbolized by the chief characteristic of Egyptian civilization: the pyramid.

In the pyramid system of organization, whoever is on top controls the system, and the rest of the pyramid supports the one who is on top. Thus, life becomes a constant struggle to get on top of the pyramid, and once you are there, the struggle is to stay on top, because all those under you are trying to knock you off so they can get on top. That was the Egypt of Moses' upbringing, but it was not the kind of system to promote community. In fact, it engendered the exact opposite of community. Yet many churches today operate on the Egyptian power system, where leadership is centralized in one person and the rest serve under him or her. This is especially seen in the small church where a patriarch or matriarch dominates the church and all decisions are made by him or her.

Some people like to belong to small churches because they desire a place where they are known. Reality declares, however, that smallness does not indicate that real community is occurring in these churches, especially if they are operating on the pyramid scheme of leadership. In fact, many larger churches have much more community occurring than some small churches. This is because they have structured their church on God's plan of community, not on the pyramid system of Egypt.

Moses indeed was schooled in this hierarchial pyramid school of control. When he discovered that God was choosing him to be Israel's deliverer, he immediately sought to accomplish deliverance through the only way he knew—by exercising power. God had to send him away to the wilderness for forty years to tend sheep and learn community instead of hierarchial power. Having learned this lesson well, he returned to Egypt, not grasping for power, but humble, teachable, and in community. Interestingly, when God sent Moses back, He did not send him alone but with his brother, Aaron, as his spokesman. He went in community with another. Leadership was now shared. That is God's plan for leadership.

In Moses' new understanding of God, God is not seen as above His people, like the Egyptian pharaohs, but rather in the midst of His people. This demonstrates the community God wishes to establish with His people. God wanted His people to have the same kind of relationship with Him that Moses had. He was not trying to establish a hierarchial priesthood. God's desire was for the entire nation to become priests (Exodus 19:5, 6). God wanted everyone to enter into a relationship with Him whereby they could all become priests. In this sense, power was dispersed among the people rather than being embodied in one person at the top, Moses.

God's initial ideal for Israel to be a kingdom of priests was abandoned when Israel rebelled at Sinai, but it is an ideal toward which God worked and finally instituted in the New Testament. The message of the priesthood of all believers does not teach that every person is a law unto himself. It indicates, instead, that Christians are to live in subjection to each other rather than seeking to dominate one another. The very nature of the doctrine demands that Christians live in community with each other.

Community is established only as leadership is diffused. Cities consolidate power for the sake of control, but God diffuses power for the sake of liberating His people into real community. Real community cannot exist in an organization which is exercising hierarchial power. The only time Pharaoh is seen in a good light in Scripture is when he gives power away, in the story of Joseph. The role of leaders interested in developing community is to give their power away. It has been suggested that God's model of leadership is the circle rather than the pyramid.

> The pyramid suggests that humanity may lift itself into heaven. The circle suggests that God must come down to earth. In the pyramid, only one person at a time can be on the top. In the circle, everyone is included as egalitarian members of the community.[6]

As we consider the structure of most churches today, we quickly recognize that most are built on the scheme of the pyramid rather than the circle. In the circle, leadership is dispersed. Hierarchial churches dare not allow small groups to function, because they fear that they cannot control them. The fear of the loss of control is the greatest hindrance to the establishment of small group ministry in most churches today. This fear of loss of control also stands behind the failure of most churches to initiate lay ministry and empower laity in ministry. It is also the reason that conferences are afraid of starting lay churches that they cannot control. This is a real issue, but somehow we must find a way to hold people and churches accountable without worrying so much about control. Surely we can trust Christ to control His church, for our human attempts to do so only create a church that is out of control. It is only through giving away power to the people that the church can become a true reflection of God, who continually gives away power. The ultimate example of this is the Incarnation, when God became flesh and lived among us.

The ministry of small groups is not just another program added to the multitude of other programs already existing in the church. Small groups are to be the central organizing principle upon which the church is built. In this way, power is released to the laity, and the church ceases to be a clerical movement. The model of church where the pastor is in control came from the apostasy of the Middle Ages, transported there directly from the pyramid structure of Egypt. It is time to return to the apostolic model of church, where the clergy empower the laity and release them for ministry. The small group is one avenue for the accomplishment of the priesthood of all believers in ministry for Christ. This was the kind of organization Jesus wished to establish when He began the Christian church. It is certainly the kind of organization needed today in the grand climax of the work of Christ's church. As Icenogle has said:

> Small groups are to be circles of mutual priesthood, where power is shared and care is recipro-

cated as every member of the group defers allegiance to God in their midst.[7]

The Jethro Model

Exodus 18:1 through 19:6 describes the situation in the camp of Israel when Jethro visited the camp and Zipporah was reunited with Moses, her husband. Jethro immediately noticed a major problem with Moses' leadership style. Moses had reverted to the pyramid style of leadership with which he had grown up. Sadly, this is the natural reaction of most leaders. It takes constant vigilance to follow God's model of leadership. As a result, Moses was exhausted and had no time for his family, and the people were not in community with each other or with God. Moses was spending all his time settling disputes among the people. He was acting like many pastors today who spend all their time ministering to the people, caring for them, and creating a congregation totally dependent upon the minister. We haven't learned anything in more than three thousand years!

Jethro's suggestion was very simple, but it was the opposite of the group leadership theory taught in those days and today. Jethro said that Moses should give away his power by empowering his people. He was to do this in such a way that no person would be in charge of more than ten people or families. That reduced power down to the size of what we today call a small group. Genuine biblical leadership empowers people at the "lowest" levels.

The result for Moses was freedom to deal with the major problems. It prevented him from being burned out, and it freed the people by empowering them to solve their own problems. The Jethro model is still a very good ministry model for the church today. Instead of the pastor being the primary caregiver in the church, the pastor releases the role of caregiver to his people, who care for each other. Such a system of caring for people does a better job than any pastor alone can do adequately.

God's plan for community is the answer for burned out, frustrated clergy of today. Give away power by empowering your people. When you delegate something to someone, don't stand over them to make certain they do it your way. Free them and trust them. The more pastors can empower their people, the more "sane" their lives will be and the more spiritually attuned their people will be.

The purpose of small groups is to give away power, to give away the priesthood. Decentralization means giving away the priesthood. On this basis churches need to evaluate their small group structure. It is not enough just to have small groups. The wrong kind of groups can create more problems than they solve. The small groups must be places where power is dispersed among the people. Does the small group ministry in your church give away power or does it use even the small groups to control people? Genuine small groups that build community give away power rather than centralizing it in the pastor or other controlling person in the church. Leaders who give the priesthood away will have more time for their families. It was stress and overwork that caused Moses to accept this new leadership system. Perhaps the high stress and long hours most pastors experience today will cause them to reevaluate how they "do church" and consider the possibility of developing a new style of ministry, one that gives away the priesthood. When pastors do this, they will empower their people to perform ministry to each other rather than being dependent upon the pastor to be the chief performer of ministry in the congregation.

Such a system—one that gives away power—demands a support structure for its leaders. Jethro's system provided that when he instructed Moses to create rulers of tens, rulers of fifties, hundreds, and thousands. These "higher" leaders were to be the support structure for the leaders of "tens" who were the field leaders in Moses' society.

One of the major problems in initiating the ministry of the laity in today's church is that pastors attempt to place people in ministry in harmony with their giftedness, but they fail to provide the support structure needed to sustain them in their ministry. Jethro's plan to have a support person for every ten people worked fine in his day. It is certainly the minimal support needed for lay ministry accomplishment today. However, due to the complexities of our day, support people may actually be needed for every three or four persons in ministry. Of course, this involves more people in ministry, but it does create a ministry of mutual support rather than all small group leaders reporting to the pastor, which is Moses' pyramid scheme of control. This simply does not work, even in small group ministry.

A circular style of leadership operating in a church today will provide a support base for all leaders. As church members recognize that power is not centralized in one person, they will become more willing to help each other solve problems. "My" problem then becomes the problem of the community, as we recognize that we are all in this together.

In the Jethro model, Moses went from being the one who passed judgment to being one who oversaw the judgment of others. As churches adopt the Jethro model of leadership, they will change, so that instead of the pastor being the chief caregiver and decision maker in the church, leadership is diffused among the people, and all the people of God are empowered for ministry. The church indeed must become a priesthood of all believers.

Old Testament and Small Groups

The Jethro model had a lasting effect on Israel throughout the period of the judges and later had implications in the establishment of Jewish synagogues, which could be established with ten people. Inherent in the call of God to the nation of Israel is the whole idea of diffusing leadership among the people. Israel's apostasy occurred when they copied the nations around them and developed the office of king to rule over them, contrary to God's purpose. Again we see the patience of God as He allowed Israel to develop kingship, contrary to His design. Sometimes God allows us to learn the hard way.

The early Adventist churches, as we shall see more fully in a later chapter, were not controlled by pastors. In our desire to copy the churches around us, God allowed us to stray from his ideal plan. Today, experiencing the same problems as other denominations, Adventists are beginning to wake up to the necessity of returning to God's plan for clergy and laity—an empowered laity trained by a clergy that diffuses power.

Summary

We can understand small groups from the perspective of the Old Testament only as we seek to understand the ideal of God from the beginning. We have seen that God is a small group and operates in interdependence with the other members of the Godhead. Furthermore, God created Adam and Eve for the purpose of establishing a relationship and entering into community with them. In that perfect community in Eden, they were able to be totally open to each other—to be "naked" and not ashamed. Yet as soon as they sinned, they felt "naked" and hid themselves, because sin had created brokenness in the community. Ever since the fall it has been the purpose of God to restore broken community. The way God attempted to do this in the Old Testament was through small groups, rather than the large groups that humanity's rebellion had created. The other way God worked to restore genuine community was through giving away power, as seen in the contrast between the Egyptian model and the Jethro model that God had Israel adopt.

Churches today that are interested in being redemptive communities will seek to return to the ideal of Eden. They will foster that which will diffuse leadership from the "few" to the "many." They will seek to empower people for ministry by releasing them for ministry instead of seeking to control all the ministry. They will foster small groups where people can be taught not to pass judgment on each other, but instead to create a place of openness and trust where people can truly care for each other in community. That is God's plan for humankind. It was for the reestablishment of this kind of society that Jesus entered human history, to redeem humankind from the fall and restore them to true community once again. As we examine Jesus' ministry, we will discover that the purpose of His ministry likewise was to give away power and create small groups where leaders are empowered and supported in real community.

Notes:

1. John 8:15, NASB.

2. Genesis 4:9.

3. Genesis 4:17.

4. Icenogle, Gareth, *Biblical Foundations for Small Group Ministry: An Integrational Approach* (Downers Grove, IL. InterVarsity Press, 1993) 32.

5. Gorman, 70 [quoting Charles Swindoll].

6. Icenogle, 101.

7. Ibid.

4

Reigniting the Relationally Based Church

While the Old Testament presents a theology of community as inherent in the Godhead, the New Testament gives us a better picture of how such community can be worked out practically in the day-to-day life of the church. Jesus' incarnational ministry thus forms the ideal backdrop for understanding God's plan for humans living in community with God and with one another.

As the New Testament era dawned, church as community had been lost sight of in the power struggles of the Pharisees and others who were more concerned with position than with the development of community. Hierarchial leaders had replaced circular leaders, and the struggle of attempting to be on the top of the pyramid dominated Judaism at this time.

Into this setting, Jesus appeared and built a movement based squarely on community and diffused leadership with an empowered people. Our guide here is not mere theory or conjecture; we have been given a living example of how to empower laity for ministry.

Jesus and Small Groups

For three and one half years, Jesus ministered on planet earth. At times He spoke to great multitudes, but most of His labor was with a small band of twelve, whom He called His disciples. Jesus spent these few years pouring His life into these few people—the twelve, the seventy, and the women who followed Him. Yet Jesus forever changed the world. Most churches today concentrate on the multitudes and wonder why they do not seem to make a major impact on the world around them. Perhaps it is time to look at Jesus' methodology in light of His theology of community

Jesus was not trying to win the multitudes. In fact, at times He even discouraged them from following Him. Instead, He focused on a small group of people, knowing that through them He could eventually reach the multitudes with the genuine thing. Lasting ministry is formed only through empowering people through small group ministry. The great preachers of the past who attempted to reach the multitudes without establishing small group ministry inevitably failed in securing lasting results. In contrast, John Wesley, who accompanied his preaching with the establishment of small groups, not only saw vast numbers come to faith in Christ but also to permanent discipleship.

Since Jesus initially organized His disciples into a small group, it is not strange that they established a small group church. Later in this book, we will examine the house church that was characteristic of the early church. At this point, just notice that this was the model Jesus gave them. They unabashedly followed that model. Jesus revealed that the way to reach the masses was through small groups that were experiencing genuine community. This did not exclude the preaching of the Word, but preaching was supported by the small group structure:

> The genius of Christ's ministry was that he devoted himself primarily to a few people rather than

the masses, in order that the masses could be more effectively reached with the gospel.[1]

The band of twelve was Jesus' chief organization for carrying out the Great Commission. He gave no elaborate schemes, no great organizational charts; He simply organized and trained a small group. And He changed the world. He was not concerned with building great institutions; He was concerned with building people. To Jesus, relationships were the most important thing that He talked about. The God who lives in community had now come to earth to give humankind a living demonstration of what it means for people to live together in community. The reason the early church caught relational ministry so well was that they had seen it modeled by the Master Himself.

The group of twelve had come from all kinds of dysfunctional groups and families. James and John came from a home where the mother had always pushed them to get ahead of others—to be the people in control. The Zealot party, of which Simon was a member, tried to gain control by military power. Matthew had used the power of Rome to enforce unwanted taxes on the populace. These are not the types of people we would normally seek when we want to build a community, yet Jesus chose them to demonstrate to us that even though people may come from dysfunctional groups and families, they can discover real community in Him.

Sometimes people feel that the only way to establish a good community is to get the right people in it at the beginning and keep out the dysfunctional people. Dysfunctional people can ruin groups—they can pose a real challenge. Yet Jesus' model of ministry indicates that dysfunctional people can be radically changed by the gospel so that they can experience real community. Since all of us are somewhat dysfunctional, Jesus' model gives us the hope that He can transform us into people who truly reside in community with Him and with each other.

Because of Jesus' involvement with a small group and because of His example of focusing most of His ministry on the development of that group, it is imperative that churches today be involved in small group ministry. In this way they pattern their ministry after Jesus' ministry. It is unthinkable that a church built on a Scriptural base could exist without small group ministry, when small groups were the essence of Jesus' ministerial style.

Jesus did not simply select the Twelve and develop them so that they could individually perform ministry. Most of His time was spent in attempting to develop community among them. They didn't trust each other at the beginning. They were not open and vulnerable with each other, but instead were very judgmental. Jesus had to change all that if they were going to represent the new community He was creating—the new Israel.

> The original twelve were the twelve sons of Jacob—a family. Jesus called the new twelve to be a new family. The ancient family of Jacob demonstrated significant sexual and spiritual brokenness: selling their brother into slavery and massacring whole villages of vulnerable people. The new family of Jesus was called away from such a destructive life pattern. They were to be the family of the reconciled as well as the reconciling family. They had to be small, and they had to be unique (separate) to Christ.[2]

To emphasize the community that He desired to create, Jesus used family words to describe the relationships they were to have with each other. They were to call each other "brother" and "sister." In fact, Jesus' most definitive statement on this new community is His claim in Matthew 12:

> While He was still speaking to the multitudes, behold, His mother and brothers were standing outside, seeking to speak to Him. And someone said to Him, "Behold, Your mother and Your brothers are standing outside seeking to speak to You." But He answered the one who was telling Him and said, "Who is My mother and who are My brothers?" And stretching out His hand toward His disciples, He said, "Behold, My mother and My broth-

ers! For whoever does the will of My Father who is in heaven, he is My brother and sister and mother.[3]

Jesus' new community transcended the natural family. People who are drawn to Him are to be a part of His new family. The very fact that Jesus used family terms to describe the relationships that believers were to have with each other and with Him is an indication that relationships were at the very core of these new communities. Getting on top of the pyramid had been the main focus before, but Jesus attempted to establish a new community—the restored Eden—where relationships are more important than hierarchial structure. Thus, in order to save humanity, Jesus creates community. The bonds that exist in the Christian community are to be as close as those in the natural family.

In the ministry of Jesus, we discover not individualism but community. Jesus calls people into this community. They may come as individuals, but they are immediately placed in contact with others so that community may be developed. While He was here on earth, the highest priority of Jesus in the establishment of His church was the creation of a relational community.

As Jesus ministered within this new community which He was developing, He taught the people how to relate to one another. And they were not to live in a vacuum. Jesus also sent them out to minister to others, because part of being in community is to minister outside of the community. However, Jesus did not send people into ministry alone—He sent them forth in pairs, two by two, for only community can create other communities. Single ministers create individualistic Christians who do not live in community because their mentor did not evangelize them in community.

Perhaps it is our failure to follow Jesus' "two by two" rule that has produced so many individualistic Christians. The fact that Jesus always ministered in a group and always sent forth His disciples in groups of at least two should cause us to question seriously our method of laboring solo. If we are biblical Christians, we will follow the Master's plan and labor in groups, just as Jesus taught us. Why does it seem so strange to do just as Jesus instructed us to do?

The question of finance always comes up at this point. The concern is that we cannot afford to pay the wages for two to work together. However, perhaps we should realize that we cannot afford to pay for the failure of the one who does not labor out of a community setting. Furthermore, it may be that we will need to think of a new kind of paid employee who labors in a community setting rather than the usual individualistic setting. This may mean a restructuring of the role of clergy as we move back into an apostolic paradigm.

Because we have adopted a nonbiblical role of the pastor, it has forced us, out of necessity, to create solo pastors. However, as we begin moving back to the New Testament model of ministry and no longer sense the need of each church having its own pastor, it will be easier to create "team ministries." Such an arrangement is absolutely necessary for church planting. Jesus defined "church" in the smallest possible way as a small group:

> Again I say to you, that if two of you agree on earth about anything that they may ask, it shall be done for them by My Father who is in heaven. For where two or three have gathered together in My name, there I am in their midst.[4]

It is interesting to note that Jesus declared that He would be with us specifically as we gathered in twos and threes. Jesus would manifest Himself in this community gathered in His name. All of Jesus' statements to be present with us are given in the setting of the church being in community, not as individuals. This does not, of course, deny that He is with us individually, but reveals Jesus' great desire to stress the need of relational groups. When Jesus thought of church as the gathered community, He had the small group in mind. Today we use this text in an apologetic fashion when attendance is sparse. Jesus proclaimed these words to help us understand that the small group is the very essence of church. We cannot have a church without the small group as the special place where Jesus dwells among His people.

Jesus' response to the disciples in this context suggested that there was not one who was greatest, but that "wherever two or three are gathered"— wherever there is a small group gathered in childlikeness, agreement, forgiveness, reclamation and reconciliation—Jesus in their midst would bring greatness to them together.[5]

Jesus is telling us that the small group is church, not a part of church, but the essence of church. It is this gathered community of the Twelve that becomes the church. Instead of looking at small groups as another program of the church, we need to start looking at them as if they are the church, for that is what Jesus has declared them to be. Again, do we believe Him or not?

In the modern church we look at small groups as just another program to be added. Jesus, however, envisioned the small, caring group as the church in total. The model of church He created was not one of large super churches, but of small groups who live in open and honest community with one another. This is not to say that large churches are wrong. Large churches can be effective places of ministry, provided that they are a collection of small groups. If the large church is only a large group, it is not a New Testament church. In the New Testament sense, large churches should be simply the gathering together of the many small groups that make up the church.

Jesus' Idea of Community in Small Groups

At the heart of Jesus' small group ministry is the idea of community. The small group does not exist for the sake of a small group. It is merely the vehicle for the establishment of community. Jesus recognized that the small group is the best means for the accomplishment of that goal. Throughout His ministry, Jesus was concerned that community be developed among His followers. This seems to be one of the most important tasks He attempted to accomplish. He knew that if His followers could not get along with each other, they could never bring others into the community. That is why Jesus spent so much time attempting to develop genuine community among the dysfunctional followers whom He had called into ministry.

Jesus' concern for community stems out of His relationship to the Godhead and the restoration of the image of God in humanity. If the process of redemption involves the complete restoration of humanity to the image of God, then it is imperative that community be established in the church Christ is establishing on earth. Jesus' understanding of church is in direct contrast to the American individualistic understanding of church:

> American individualism sometimes flies in the face of this when a person says, "I can worship God on my own. I don't need the church." Such a statement misses the core value and key purpose of "church" as face-to-face gathering and that God can only be known fully in community as community.[6]

There was no place for monasticism in Jesus' understanding of community. There was no room for those who wished to serve God in isolation. Some, of course, must serve in isolation by necessity, but this should never be done by choice. To Jesus, the essence of church was involvement in community, and He could not envision church in our Western individualistic understanding. Spiritual growth, Jesus knew, occurs only when people live in community with each other.

Evidently involvement in community is not an option for the Christian, it is Christianity. Adventists have been great exponents of the priesthood of all believers. It is not just part of our Reformation heritage, it is our New Testament right. We have clearly understood the priesthood to indicate each Christian's ability to go directly to God without any Mediator except Christ. However, there is another part to being a priest that we must never forget: people cannot be priests apart from the community they serve. There is no such thing as a people being priests all by themselves. To be a priest means to be in community. Since a priest is to serve others in the community, and since all believers in the community are priests, then the priesthood of all believers is a call for all Christians to minister to one another.

It is in this sense that all the "one another" passages in the New Testament become very meaningful, for they describe the ministry of the priest—a ministry of mutual care. That kind of care can only be provided in a community. Therefore the priesthood of all believers demands all such priests to live in community with each other. Anything short of this is denial of the New Testament understanding of the priesthood of all believers.

In this understanding of the new priesthood Jesus established and the small groups that became the church of the New Testament, Jesus has established a new model of church. It is a model that teaches believers to depend on one another instead of on themselves. It is the model fully developed in the house churches described in the book of Acts, which we will examine in the next chapter.

So important was the establishment of community for the New Testament church that Jesus even instructed the disciples that they should wait until the authenticating Spirit had established the church at Pentecost before they went forth to give the verbal witness of the resurrection. Only through the establishment of a community of faith can witness to the faith be adequately given. Jesus did not want to establish an individualistic gospel. He wished to establish a church where people are nurtured and witness in community. Community witness begets other communities. Inherent in Jesus' understanding of community is the need for these communities to be reproducible. Genuine, healthy communities will reproduce themselves. A small group or church, therefore, that is not reproducing itself by establishing new relational communities is an unhealthy church. Just having small groups in a church does not create community. These communities must multiply if they are healthy at the core.

It is for this purpose that Jesus is one of the greatest exponents of small groups the world has ever seen. He created the perfect group, and that group changed the world. They were not perfect when they entered the group, but through the nurture of the group they became the transformed disciples of Jesus. Jesus indicated that Christian growth cannot occur apart from involvement in group life:

> Thus the Christian community is a place where we can start to practice the Christian life together. It needs to be a place where we can succeed and fail in an atmosphere of acceptance and adherence to God's Law.[7]

It is God's plan and Jesus' desire that Christians grow in small groups. The purpose of small groups is not just meeting to study the Bible. The purpose of groups is to give Christians a place where they can grow together. If intellectual knowledge alone is being attained from Bible study, then the small group is a failure, because its true purpose is spiritual growth, not intellectual attainment.

In the pursuit of small groups in Adventism, concern has been expressed about relational groups. "Small groups are all right as long as they stick to Bible study," is what many have said. It seems that we are afraid of developing deep relationships in community with one another. Yet this is the very purpose of small groups, according to Jesus. Groups that opt only for the intellectual pursuits of Bible study are, in a certain sense, dysfunctional. We need to be in a group in order to hold each other accountable for our life in Christ, to truly care for one another, and to adequately witness for Christ. Perhaps we are fearful of relational groups because we don't want to be accountable to each other, to care for one another, or to witness. Intellectual groups are "safe." We don't have to be open and vulnerable with each other, but such groups do not create real Christians, only pseudo ones. This does not mean that growing in Bible knowledge is bad—Christians should grow in their understanding of the Word. But if intellectual knowledge is all that occurs, it is not a genuine New Testament group. New Testament groups will grow both in Bible knowledge and in relationship with one another.

Small relational groups are the heart of Christianity, and it must be the heart of the Adventist church if we are serious about being the church of Jesus—for Jesus' church is a relational church. A relational church is one of the greatest needs in a world that is starving for relationships. Likewise, the development of a relational church is one of the greatest needs of the church today. God help us to become serious about developing a relational church. The key to doing this, according to Jesus, is to establish a small group church whose members live in community with each other.

Notes:

1. John Mallison, *Growing Christians in Small Groups* (Sydney, Australia: Anzea Publishers, 1989), 3.

2. Icenogle, 207.

3. Matt. 12:46-50, NASB.

4. Matt. 18:19, 20, NASB.

5. Icenogle, 227.

6. Icenogle, 258.

7. Jeffrey Arnold, *The Big Book on Small Groups* (Downers Grove, IL: InterVarsity Press, 1992), 73, 74.

5

Pentecost Establishes the Relational Church

Throughout His ministry, Jesus had modeled to His disciples a church that was relational, where people lived together in community as they were being restored from the brokenness of humanity. Out of this family community, evangelism was to occur. With the explosion of Holy Spirit power at Pentecost, the church grew in numbers as well as in spirituality. What was this new community of believers like? Was it just a large group of people who met together once a week to worship God? Note the biblical testimony of life in the earliest Christian community, the church at Jerusalem immediately after Pentecost:

> So then, those who had received his word were baptized; and there were added that day about three thousand souls. And they were continually devoting themselves to the apostles' teaching and to fellowship, to the breaking of bread and to prayer.[1]

When the three thousand were baptized, they immediately became involved in four things: study, fellowship, food, and prayer. They were not only involved, but Scripture declares that they were devoted to these four things. Two of the four, food and fellowship, are unquestionably group activities. Since these two require a small group setting, it is probably safe to assume that the other two activities, teaching and prayer, also occurred in a small group setting.

This would suggest that the earliest church, immediately after Pentecost, was already divided into small groups. While three thousand became disciples at once, they very quickly are seen partaking of small group activities. How did they get so well organized so quickly? Probably because dividing people into small groups was the plan Jesus had demonstrated to them. The pattern that Jesus had used, now duplicated in the disciples' ministry, reveals again that ministering to people in small groups is a vital part of the divine plan. Many times they had seen Jesus, after speaking to the multitudes, divide the people into groups and then let the disciples share with them and answer their questions. Since this was the method Jesus taught them, it is not surprising that they immediately organized the fledgling church into groups.

This small group life is seen as the church continues to grow both spiritually and numerically:

> And all those who had believed were together, and had all things in common; and they began selling their property and possessions, and were sharing them with all, as anyone might have need. And day by day, continuing with one mind in the temple, and breaking bread from house to house, they were taking their meals together with gladness and sincerity of heart.[2]

Here we discover that the sharing of food was done in homes, which implies that the believers did not all meet in one place but in many different homes. The logistics of finding a place in Jerusalem where over three thousand people could meet together every day would have been difficult, if not impossible. Evidently the three thousand were immediately divided into small groups, where they were nurtured and nourished by the hundred and twenty.

The church established at Pentecost did not meet only as a large body in one place. It immediately became a small group church. The presence of three thousand or more people meeting in one place in Jerusalem every day would have created a strong political unit that would have had to be reckoned with. That might have seemed advantageous at the time to the politically motivated disciples, but Jesus had given them a model to follow. That model was not only a large body, but also small groups. In obedience to the Master, they immediately created a small group structure in the church. It was impossible to be a Christian in the early church without being a part of a small group. Small groups were the building block upon which the early believers established their church.

The small group activities of the early church consisted of four things: study of the teachings of Jesus, which they learned from the apostles; fellowship; breaking of bread; and prayer. These are all small group activities. In the small group setting the early church did Bible study. With few people present, it was not one-way conversation but dialogue, where the believers could ask questions. While no doubt didactic teaching occurred, it was in a strong small group setting.

This does not mean that meeting in large groups is wrong. The early church had large meetings as well. However, the large meetings seem to be evangelistic in nature rather than occurring for the weekly or daily nurture of the saints. Once people came to Christ, they seem to have met regularly in a small group rather than in a large preaching meeting. Clearly, the foundation of the early church was laid in a small group structure rather than in large groups.

The second aspect of life in the early church was fellowship. The believers didn't just gather to study and then leave. Intermingled with their study was time for fellowship. The form of the fellowship is not spelled out in Scripture, but the results are clear. The book of Acts declares that they shared everything in common. Somehow through the teaching that was shared, they saw the immediate need of providing for one another. Believers willingly sold their own possessions in order to help fellow believers. This is the closest possible kind of fellowship. Jesus had taught that the church was to be a new family, a community that healed the brokenness of humankind. The fellowship operating in this early church demonstrated that the teachings of Jesus were at work. Scripture declares that "they had all things in common." Theirs was a totally open society. The "hiddenness" of fallen Eden had been removed, and the believers could openly share their doubts, their struggles, their problems. There was no judgmentalism, but true care for one another. All the aspects of dysfunctional community that had been rampant in the world were being removed in the fellowship of these early Christians. Indeed, fellowship was at the very heart and center of what it meant to be a Christian in the early church.

The third aspect of life in the early church was that they ate together. One of the best ways for groups to bond is to eat together. It goes hand in hand with fellowship. So great was the fellowship in the early church that these believers ate together every day. This breaking of bread was done in the homes; it was not a large meeting with a symbolic breaking of bread. This was real fellowship with shared food.

The fourth and final aspect of life in the early church is described as prayer time. Not only did the people study, fellowship, and eat together; they also prayed together. Praying together in groups builds strong community and spirituality. As people openly share their prayer needs with each other, the group becomes closely cemented. Even today we notice that we draw closer to those with whom we pray regularly. Since prayer occurred in small groups every day, we can easily imagine that this activity pulled the early believers into the closest harmony.

What happened in the book of Acts immediately after Pentecost has been called the birth of the church, and rightly so, but many people have not understood what kind of church was established. Many have thought it to be a large church meeting together as one group. Few have given thought to the type of church brought forth by the Pentecost event. As we have seen, it was a church where the Holy Spirit scattered the believers into various small groups. Within these groups they could build the kind of church Jesus had envisioned, a community in Christ where people really cared for each other. This is the New Testament church of the book of Acts. It is not a church with small groups, but a church that is small groups. Real fellowship was occurring in this church. The Greek word translated here is koinonia. This word expresses the closest kind of fellowship occurring among the disciples:

> But koinonia expresses something new and independent. It denotes the unanimity and unity brought about by the Spirit. The individual was completely upheld by the community.[3]

Community had been restored. The brokenness of the fall had been restored. Jesus' mission to heal that which was broken, to free that which was bound (Luke 4:18), had been accomplished in the church established by Pentecost. The brokenness of humanity was in the process of being healed through the healthy communities being established by the apostles. The believers cared so much for each other that they willingly sold their property to help provide for the common good. Not since the fall had such healthy communities existed on this planet. These redemptive communities were established not by human ingenuity but by the divine Spirit of God. The Spirit helped the early believers to establish small group churches where it was possible for healing and restoration to occur. Truly this was a work of God in the midst of His people.

Some may have entertained the idea that the early church met in homes because of the persecution that was occurring. However, in the earliest days, Christianity was regarded as a sect of Judaism and therefore was not outlawed. That occurred later. It was true that Christians were persecuted by Jews, but there seems to be nothing secret about the meetings of the believers. Three thousand people meeting daily in homes in one city would be difficult to hide. Even though the authorities would not know their numbers as easily as if they met in one place, they still knew they were a sizeable group.

The reason for small group meetings was not just political. The disciples could have found several small halls where they could have met, but they chose homes, which limited the number of believers in each location. This writer believes that they deliberately chose homes as meeting places to limit the size of each group so that real community could take place. Even the well-to-do homes of the first century in Jerusalem could hold only about thirty people.[4] And these were the upper-income homes. Few homes would have met even these specifications, which means that most churches would have consisted of fewer than thirty. Many, no doubt, numbered only ten or fifteen. Such innumerable meeting places could very quickly give the impression that Christians were everywhere. And they were!

Evidently the believers learned something from the teachings of Jesus that caused them to develop a church centered in homes rather than in large gatherings. Jesus even inaugurated the last supper in a home.

Why did Christians choose to meet in homes? Because Jesus had modeled that kind of community setting, and they simply followed His example. As Robert Banks has observed, the family character of the early church called for meetings to be held in homes, because homes provided these early Christians with the most conducive atmosphere to give expression to the faith that they held in common.[5]

While the early church sometimes may have met together in one place, such meetings seem to have been the exception rather than the rule. The normal place for these meetings was the home. As Christianity was established throughout the Roman empire, the home continued to be the primary meeting place of the early church. This forced the church to stay small and multiply new groups as it grew rather than to centralize. For the first three hundred years of the Christian era, the church met in homes. Special meeting places were not built for more than three hundred years, and even these were small in comparison to the large structures later developed.

While the church in Jerusalem and elsewhere consisted of many small groups meeting throughout the city, the groups were not independent of each other. They still comprised one church. At times the various groups met together; however, their real life occurred in the small group. The twelve apostles were the common link that bound the various groups together. While each group was bound to the others, they still were a complete community on their own. They did not need to meet with the larger group in order to be the church, for Jesus had declared that where two or three are gathered in His name, He is present. That would make each of these house fellowships a church in the fullest sense, even though they were also linked to the larger body. All would be part of the one fellowship that all enjoyed in Christ, but the closest fellowship occurred as believers met together in individual homes.

This early Jerusalem church had both a centralized leadership in the twelve apostles and a decentralized leadership in the small groups that existed all over the city. How they were interconnected is not made plain in Scripture. But we know that the earliest church was primarily a small group church. Leaders for these small house groups had to be trained rapidly to fit the needs of the expanding church. One thing is clear, and that is that the church continued to expand its groups as its membership increased.

The book of Acts makes clear that the church initially produced by the Pentecost event was centered in small group fellowship. Such a setting for the church continued for nearly three hundred years, until the church was institutionalized at the time of Constantine. The amazing thing is that the church was able to multiply and grow most rapidly without buildings, without institutions, and even without mass meetings. The church centered in community was the norm for

Christians of the first three hundred years.

Before or during and with or without persecution, active participation in a house church was not considered an option—it was the norm![6]

Another factor that cannot be ignored is that these house churches became the center of all Christian activity. As the church spread beyond Jerusalem, the early leaders would start a church, train the elders to care for it, and then leave. The home churches had to provide their own care. No pastors were imposed from outside. An institutionalized church with large numbers meeting in one place could not have provided the necessary nurture. It had to be decentralized, and the home small group meeting was ideal. This church could truly reflect the community of Christ and not tie up the resources of the church in maintaining a spiritually healthy congregation. Clergy were free to continue planting new groups of believers all over the world, training them in the small group setting to be communities of faith which administered mutual care.

Today the church has departed from the New Testament norm. Our institutional churches fail to provide community, and we spurn the house church as a relic of days gone by. Yet the modern small group movement may help us to revitalize and reestablish this forgotten part of the mission of Christ. The principle we gather from the early church is that the church of Jesus is to be a church that exists in community, not in buildings, programs, and large group meetings.

It is time to rediscover our roots and return the church to its apostolic heritage—a church built on the foundation laid by Christ and the apostles. This church is truly in community; its people provide care for each other in small group settings. In the new Testament era, small groups were not an option; neither can they be an option for the church of the twenty-first century. It is time to redesign the local church around small groups and return to the early church model of ministry.

Notes:

1. Acts 2:41, 42, NASB.

2. Acts 2:44-46, NASB.

3. Colin Brown, ed., *The New International Dictionary,* Vol 1 (Grand Rapids, MI: Zondervan, 1971), 642.

4. Robert Banks, *Paul's Idea of Community* (Peabody, MA: Hendrikson Publishers, 1996) 35.

5. Ibid, 56.

6. Neal F. McBride, *How to Lead Small Groups* (Colorado Springs, CO: NavPress, 1990), 19.

6

Paul Plants Relational Churches Everywhere

Since most of the book of Acts details the ministries of the apostle Paul, we have chosen to examine Paul's ministry in this separate chapter. In the previous chapter we have looked at only the beginnings of the Christian church at the Pentecost event. In this chapter we will examine Paul's ministry as outlined in Acts and in the epistles.

The apostle Paul was the greatest exporter of Christianity in the first century. His missionary journeys established Christianity all over the Roman world. Examining the kind of church Paul established will help us understand the beginnings of Christianity more clearly and discover whether the relational church established at Pentecost was a passing fad or a permanent structure inherent in the theology of the apostles.

It becomes abundantly clear as one examines Paul's writings that the Pentecost event had set the norm for the Holy Spirit–empowered church that developed in the first century. What began at Pentecost continued throughout the apostolic era. The apostle Paul continued to plant churches on the Pentecostal model rather than on the institutional model. The institutional model of the church that we operate on today was unknown in the experience of the earliest church. It is not that the model was not in existence, for Judaism had clearly degenerated into an institutional church when Christianity began. If the apostles had copied any system, it would probably have been the Jewish religious system, with which they would have been very familiar. Instead, they chose to create an entirely new system, one based on community rather than on institutional structure. That was what Jesus had taught them, and Pentecost had authenticated His teaching and led to the establishment of a relational church, built on community in small groups.

Only Jesus had more influence on the formation of the Christian church than did the apostle Paul. His writings consume fully one third of the New Testament, and most of the earliest churches planted in Asia were a result of his labors. Therefore, his influence on the formation of the Christian church is foundational and must be examined very carefully.

In obedience to Christ's instruction to go two by two, Paul began his missionary journeys in community with other disciples. Sometimes it was Paul, Barnabas, and Mark—other times he was accompanied by Silas. Paul and his company did not seek simply to disciple individuals but continually sought to reach the *oikos* of those they evangelized.[1] The early church practiced team ministry. There were no solo workers in the first-century churches, because evangelism was always done in community, as Jesus commanded. It takes community to create community. Solo workers produce institutions and not communities. That's why "two by two," the smallest community, is given by Jesus as the smallest evangelistic team. Never does Jesus send people out alone. Yet evangelism in the twentieth century has become a solo affair, with individuals working alone to win souls one by one. Perhaps we today need to listen again to Jesus' command and go out two by two.[2]

Evangelism in first-century Christianity was always done by a community and focused on a community. The reason for this was that Christ had commissioned a new community, and He had modeled community evangelism throughout His ministry. The early disciples could not help themselves—they were trained by Jesus, and they practiced what they had been taught. In the model of the early church, there is no Christianity without a community. Neither can one be a Christian if one is not part of the community.

In our modern world many people think it is possible to be a Christian and not be a part of a Christian community, a church. They feel that they can worship God apart from association with the church. Such a concept is totally foreign to New Testament Christians, who perceived the church as community. Of course, just belonging to the church does not guarantee that one has become a part of the community, but it is impossible to have community in isolation. Notice Robert Banks' insightful comments on how Paul has tied salvation with belonging to the community:

> Already we see how closely Paul's understanding of freedom, or salvation, is bound up with his idea of community. He does not view salvation as simply a transaction between the individual and God. Prior to their encounter with Christ people belong to a community, however much their actions incline them to pursue their own (or their immediate circle's) self-interest. And it is into a new community that their reconciliation with God in Christ brings them, however much they experience that event as an individual affair.[3]

> To embrace the gospel, then, is to enter into community. A person cannot have one without the other.[4]

Thus Paul established churches designed to be communities. They were not mighty fortresses or large cathedrals. They were small house churches where individuals could enter into real community with other Christians. This was no accident. It was a deliberate strategy of Paul in obedience to the model of Christ. Paul's church planting strategy was in direct line with what the Holy Spirit had accomplished at Pentecost in establishing the relational church.

Paul's most definitive statement on community is found in the parallel passages of Rom. 12 and 1 Cor. 12, where he discusses spiritual gifts in the setting of the unity of the community of Christ. Note one of the key verses from these passages:

> For just as we have many members in one body and all the members do not have the same function, so we, who are many, are one body in Christ, and individually members one of another.[5]

Here Paul emphatically declares that all Christians are members of one body—they exist in community with each other. All may function differently according to their gifts, but they are mutually dependent on each other. There is no room here for isolated Christians. To be a Christian, according to Paul, is to be in community with other Christians. Believers were not to be simply members of a body, however. In that body they were also members "one of another." It was not just membership in a body that concerned Paul, but that the believer be brought into mutual dependence upon others in the community. If Paul is correct, then individuals who are members of churches but are not living in community with other Christians, mutually dependent upon each other, are not really Christians in the New Testament sense. To be a Christian is to be included in a group that provides care for each other. Any group that is not this kind of mutually caring community is not Christ's church, no matter what its claims to truth may be. Truth is more than correct belief, as important as that may be. Truth must also be seen in the lives of those who have accepted Christ and who are living in obedience to Him. Such obedience demands that Christians live in mutual dependence on each other. This is the heart of Paul's understanding of community. Note Paul's description of this caring community:

Let love be without hypocrisy. Abhor what is evil; cling to what is good. Be devoted to one another in brotherly love; give preference to one another in honor; not lagging behind in diligence, fervent in spirit, serving the Lord; rejoicing in hope, persevering in tribulation, devoted to prayer, contributing to the needs of the saints, practicing hospitality. Bless those who persecute you; bless and curse not. Rejoice with those who rejoice, and weep with those who weep. Be of the same mind toward one another; do not be haughty in mind, but associate with the lowly. Do not be wise in your own estimation. Never pay back evil for evil to anyone. Respect what is right in the sight of all men. If possible, so far as it depends on you, be at peace with all men.[6]

Paul's understanding of community is very clear in this passage. It is at the heart of all the "one another" passages in the New Testament. The "one another" passages actually arise out of Paul's theological understanding of community. It is in this community that real care for each other occurs. Christians are not called to serve God singularly but in community with other people, where they can care for each other, love each other, rejoice with each other. These are the hallmarks of genuine Christian community.

In 1 Cor. 12, Paul continues to discuss spiritual giftedness in the church. The Spirit may give gifts to people individually, but the gifts are not to be used independently. They are to be used in the community. According to Paul, if all Christians are using their spiritual gifts, the church will be complete. No one individual has all the gifts. That's why community is needed, for the sharing of the gifts, which will create the "completeness" of the body. If one member fails to use his or her gifts, the body suffers, just as the human body suffers when it is missing a hand. The body continues to exist, but it cannot function as effectively as it does when all the parts are functioning together. That is the essence of Paul's vision of the church: a body, with different functioning members, working together harmoniously with Christ as the head. Note again Paul's argument:

> For even as the body is one and yet has many members, and all the members of the body, though they are many, are one body, so also is Christ. For by one Spirit we were all baptized into one body, whether Jews or Greeks, whether slaves or free, and we were all made to drink of one Spirit. For the body is not one member, but many.[7]

Here is the heart of Paul's theology of community. Christians are actually baptized into the body. There is no hint here of being baptized without becoming a part of the community. Today we see people being baptized and not being made a part of any Christian community. This would be heresy to Paul. Baptism was the rite by which a believer joined the community. In New Testament Christianity one could not be baptized without becoming a part of the community. Note however, that what Paul envisions here is not just church membership, but participation in a community, which he has already defined in Rom. 12 as being mutually dependent and caring. After detailing the "body" example in verses 15-21, Paul clearly espouses the idea that part of being in community is to care for those who are the weakest:

> On the contrary, it is much truer that the members of the body which seem to be weaker are necessary; and those members of the body, which we deem less honorable, on these we bestow more abundant honor, and our unseemly members come to have more abundant seemliness, whereas our seemly members have no need of it. But God has so composed the body, giving more abundant honor to that member which lacked.[8]

Paul's idea of community is that those members of the community who are the weakest are to receive special attention. They are the objects of special care and more extensive labor. This care and labor is not to be performed by the pastor of the church but by the other members. The idea of hiring someone to provide care would be such an anathema to Paul that he would declare it to be heresy and an abandonment of the essence of the Christianity that Jesus established. Care of members for each other is a body function, not something that can be hired out. To be in Christ is to be a part of a community where members care for each other. All passages in the New Testament addressing the care of existing Christians are always addressed to the whole body, never to a hired individual. The New Testament says a lot about nurture and care, but always in the context of mutual caring for one another. This mutual care is necessary to sustain spiritual life. If we hire someone to provide this care, we lose out on the spiritual strength "caring" is meant to give us. That's why it must remain a body function. Paul concludes this passage with a very clear description of what this community looks like:

> . . . that there should be no division in the body, but that the members should have the same care for one another. And if one member suffers, all the members suffer with it; if one member is honored, all the members rejoice with it. Now you are Christ's body, and individually members of it.[9]

Paul's two classic passages on community reinforce our understanding that Paul's theology is consistent with Jesus' idea of community. Jesus came to form a new community where people truly cared for each other. The early believers established house churches that were small enough that people could know and care for each other. Paul the theologian gives us the theological background to understand why the church formed small group churches. The reason that house churches were formed was not just that they provided a convenient place to meet or that the membership was too small to have larger facilities. The formation of house churches came in response to the theology of community as espoused first by Jesus and then by Paul. Only in small groups could people come to know each other well enough for real community to develop. The development of the small group

New Testament church was not an accident, it was by divine design.

If we have perceived Paul's theology correctly, then it is imperative that the church today design a church based on small groups of people who live in community with each other. This means that we must not simply have small groups in our churches, but these small groups must be the biblical community. This could mean the establishment of house churches, but it does not have to. Larger churches can accomplish community if they are divided into smaller groups. For this to happen, the local church leadership and pastor must be willing to give away power to the groups and their leaders. This is frightening, but it is biblical.

In most churches today, joining a small group is an option. This can no longer be our practice. While transition will be slow, if the church is serious about following Christ's instruction, it must restore community. That necessitates reestablishing the church as a collage of small groups where people truly care for each other. Attending meetings of the large group may be optional, but being involved in small groups cannot. Today involvement in a large group on Sabbath morning is considered the mandatory obligation of Christians and involvement in small groups, in most churches, is considered optional. This understanding must be reversed if the church is to follow the New Testament model. There were times when all the house churches in one city came together, as implied in 1 Cor. 14:23, but the implication is that the church comprised small house churches all over the city and only occasionally came together as a large group.

If the early church consisted primarily of small groups, it would imply an entirely different way of "doing church" than is currently practiced in most churches today, where the primary and chief activity of the church is the assembling of the believers at Sabbath morning worship. In the typical church, the pattern is the same whether five people are present or five hundred. Parishioners sit in pews or chairs facing the pulpit. They look at the back of people's heads and listen in silence as a pastor presents a sermon. They may sing a few songs, but worship is more of a spectator sport than an activity they engage in.

In such a setting it is possible to attend without ever speaking to another person. There is no community. Yet Christianity is community. It is true that many people find community in the church. However, it is not usually found in the worship service, but in activities held outside of worship or in fellowship they enjoy before or after the service. Since most people leave right after the worship service, very few are finding real community on Sabbath. The result is that precious few people are really finding the community Jesus so ardently desired His followers to possess. The present situation has arisen because we have defined, as the chief religious obligation, attendance on Sabbath morning rather than involvement in community.

Other people feel that the reason the church exists is to worship God. Thus we do not attend church to find fellowship but to worship. Therefore we should be silent and worship God during the hour of worship, leaving fellowship for other times. It may be true that the church exists to worship God, but the fault here is in the definition of "worship." Is worship simply being silent in church? Such a theology is foreign to the New Testament. Actually, the New Testament church did not meet to worship God, but for fellowship! Jesus gave us a new understanding of worship in His discussion with the woman at the well of Samaria:

> Jesus said to her, "Woman, believe Me, an hour is coming when neither in this mountain, nor in Jerusalem, shall you worship the Father. You worship that which you do not know; we worship that which we know, for salvation is from the Jews. But an hour is coming, and now is, when the true worshipers shall worship the Father in spirit and truth; for such people the Father seeks to be His worshipers. God is spirit, and those who worship Him must worship in spirit and truth.[10]

Place is no longer to be important in Christian worship. People don't have to go to a sacred place in order to worship. True worship is defined as obedience to Christ in every act of life. Worship is not something people do once a week on Sabbath morning but is an activity people engage in throughout the week. Worship is the life of obedience that people live for the Master. Paul further elaborates on this new theology of worship:

> I urge you therefore, brethren, by the mercies of God, to present your bodies a living and holy sacrifice, acceptable to God, which is your spiritual service of worship.[11]

Paul elaborates on Jesus' embryonic teaching of worship by declaring that the entire life of the Christian is worship. It is the ministry that individual Christians do for the Master in harmony with their spiritual gifts. Spiritual gifts ministry, according to Paul, is real worship. In fact, an understanding of worship as the utilization of the spiritual gifts appears at the beginning of Paul's main theological passage describing the church as a community. Therefore, according to Paul, the church does not meet to worship God; rather, it worships God in all that the members do. This does not mean that people do not worship when they go to church. But they worship there only because that is part of their life, and everything they do in life is worship. Therefore it is a misnomer to refer to the main activity of the church as a "worship service." Such a concept distorts the true biblical understanding of worship and reduces it to an activity of the institutional church rather than the obedience of life.

The idea of a worship service being the chief function of the church is a relic of the Dark Ages. Unwittingly, we again have accepted the apostasy of the past as the Christian norm and have lost sight of the fact that real worship is the obedience of life. The church in apostasy first made institutional worship the norm; the ultimate result was the establishment of an hour of worship as the only requirement for Christians. Could Adventism be headed down the same path by elevating the worship service as the chief function of Christians? The ultimate end is an hour a week with God. Christianity must affect the entire life, not just one hour a week! In Paul's understanding of worship, people did not meet in church simply for the purpose of worship—they came for fellowship. In the process of fellowshiping, they indeed worshiped God. Fellowship is worship. Everything the Christian does, Paul declares, is worship. To Paul, the focal point of local churches would not be the worship service at eleven o'clock on Sabbath morning but the relationships that occurred in the fellowship.

If fellowship is the biblical rationale for the church meeting together, then the church must be composed of small fellowship groups where individuals can find community with one another. The idea that the large meeting of the church is the primary place where Christians assemble must change. This does not mean that large meetings are not necessary or important, but that they are not to be the primary place of Christian assemblage, for people do not find community in such large gatherings. In fact, the large gatherings are meaningful only when relationships have been built up in the small group meetings of the church.

What did the early church do when it met together? Unfortunately, the New Testament does not give us a detailed account. We have only a few indications. Acts 2:42 indicates four main activities of the church as it assembled: they devoted themselves to the apostles' teaching (Bible study), fellowship, breaking of bread, and prayer. Paul indicates in Eph. 5:19 and again in Col. 3:16 that these gatherings included singing of psalms, hymns, and spiritual songs. It should be noted that these are all communal activities, not spectator activities. There seems to be no indication in the New Testament period of a preacher regularly presenting sermons to a congregation. Preaching is almost always seen in the context of evangelistic presentations to non-Christians. It is only on rare occasion (Acts 20:7) that New Testament congregations are recorded as listening to preaching as part of their regular assemblage.

Since this is an argument from silence, it does not mean

that preaching did not occur or that it is wrong for a church to have preaching. It simply means that there is no record of this being a part of the regular activity of the early church. However, it does seem strange that the church today has made preaching the central focus of Christian worship in light of the fact that it is not even mentioned as a regular part of New Testament worship. Preaching was vital, necessary, and used extensively in reaching non-Christians; it was for the sharing of the good news, not for the maintenance of the saints.

Lest the reader assume that the author is suggesting that we abandon all Bible study and preaching and become totally relational as a church, let me state clearly that the early church did study the apostles' teaching and were devoted to it. The church must never neglect the study of the Word. The argument presented here for relational experiences when the church assembles is an argument for an addition to what is currently done, rather than a replacement. The church must minister to people both cognitively and relationally. Adventists have not erred on the cognitive side, but we have erred greatly by neglecting the relational aspect. In the final chapter some suggestions will be offered to help our church move closer to a biblical practice of Christians meeting together.

The apostle Paul has expanded our understanding of Jesus' model of community as the norm for the Christian church. He has given us a theological basis and a practical model for such a community in the churches he established. Paul worked in community with others; he won people in groups (communities) and then placed the new believers in the new communities he established. He then modeled and developed a pattern of church radically different from the Jewish worship of his time. He did so by transforming the church from a spectator to a participatory activity. Church under Paul's leadership became not a service one attended but a fellowship one entered.

Notes:

1. Acts 16:15, 31-33.

2. Mark 6:7; Luke 10:1.

3. Banks, 17.

4. Ibid., 27.

5. Rom. 12:4, 5, NASB.

6. Rom. 12:9-18, NASB.

7. 1 Cor. 12:12-14, NASB.

8. 1 Cor. 12:22-24, NASB.

9. 1 Cor. 12:25-27, NASB.

10. John 4:21-24, NASB.

11. Rom. 12:1, NASB.

7

The Purpose of Evangelism

It was not only Jesus and Paul who emphasized Christianity as community; this, as we have seen, was inherent in the practice of the New Testament church itself. The study of Jesus and Paul consumes the bulk of the New Testament writings. However, in the few books written outside of Paul and the gospels, there is also evidence of community as the essence of Christianity. Perhaps the most definitive statement on community comes from the apostle John, the one who lived in closest community with Jesus:

> What was from the beginning, what we have heard, what we have seen with our eyes, what we beheld and our hands handled, concerning the Word of Life—and the life was manifested, and we have seen and bear witness and proclaim to you the eternal life, which was with the Father and was manifested to us— what we have seen and heard we proclaim to you also, that you also may have fellowship with us; and indeed our fellowship is with the Father, and with His Son Jesus Christ. And these things we write, so that our joy may be made complete.[1]

81

The reason for preaching the gospel of Jesus Christ, according to John, is to establish community. It was not just to save people individually, but that they might have fellowship with those who already lived in fellowship with the Father and His Son. Just as the Father and Son exist in community with the church Christ has established, so those who join themselves to Christ exist in community with others who have already been brought into community.

The purpose of our evangelism is to bring people into community. If all we do is to bring people to a knowledge of salvation and truth but fail to bring them into community, we have failed in our Christian mission. Here again John is in agreement with Jesus and Paul. The church is not a building; it is not a creed—it is a fellowship. It exists for the sake of bringing other people into its fellowship. Yet it is a fellowship not just of individuals, but of individuals who are also in fellowship with the Father and the Son.

John has declared that the vertical fellowship and the horizontal fellowship cannot be separated. If we live in fellowship with the Father and Son, we will live in fellowship with one another. Here is a return to the original idea of community in Genesis, when God, who lived in community with the Son and the Spirit, increased the community by creating Adam and Eve to live in eternal fellowship with the Godhead. Sin broke that relationship, but now, through Jesus, it has been restored. Just as God created Adam and Eve to increase His fellowship, so we proclaim Christ for the purpose of increasing this fellowship. The expansion of fellowship by the act of creation is now accomplished through the acceptance of the act of redemption.

Fellowships therefore exist for the purpose of reproduction—to create other fellowships. Navel-gazing fellowships that do not reproduce are leeches on the system. Healthy groups will reproduce regularly. Any group (a small group or even a church) that is not regularly reproducing is neither healthy nor a biblical fellowship. Inherent in the "DNA" that God placed in the first group is the urge to go forth and "multiply."

Fellowship with Christ is impossible without fellowship with other Christians. John has declared that if we walk in the light, we have fellowship with one another, and the result is that the blood of Christ cleanses us from sin. Even the cleansing from sin occurs in community. 1 John 1:7 has declared that only as we walk in the light and enter into mutual fellowship with other Christians does the blood of Christ cleanse us from sin. Those who are cleansed are placed in community, because only in community can we be held accountable for not repeating those sins.

Yet most Christians shy away today from groups that require accountability. We are so afraid of our image that we don't even want our friends to see that we are still sinners in need of the pardoning grace of Christ. So we hide behind our masks and pretend to be what we are not. John's statement stands in stark contrast to the hiddenness of modern Christians. God has saved us into a community of fellow sinners so that we can be accountable to each other. We are not to judge each other, but to help each other in our mutual struggles with sin. We are not to be in this battle alone. That's why we are saved into a community.

The passage in 1 John is perhaps one of the most definitive statements on the purpose of the church found anywhere in Scripture. The very reason for the existence of the church is the establishment of community, or fellowship. Fellowship is thus not a sideline of Christian activity, but biblically it is the essence of what it means to be a Christian. One cannot be a Christian in isolation from others. "It is not good for man to be alone." God created us to live in communities of mutual dependence upon one another.

One of the chief ways that community can be created in the modern church is through small groups. Christians who belong to large churches today can still find the fellowship Christ envisioned for His church if they also belong to a small group. Not that the small group is the panacea for all church problems. There are good groups and bad groups, but community cannot be found apart from a group. Groups can create both good and bad communities. Adventist churches should be helping people discover good communities, since there are so many bad communities in the world. There is no question that people will live in community. It is part of our nature. The need is for the church to become a truly loving, caring community. The small group is the best vehicle to accomplish this. However, simply being in a small group is not the answer, because there may not be any community in that particular group. We must help people enter into community. Therefore Adventist churches today need to create small groups that are truly community and enable people to find fellowship in these groups.

The small group is the ideal place for Jesus to fulfill His ultimate desire for transforming people. He does not transform them individually as much as He does in groups. The community is the place for transformation. Therefore the community must be a place where it is safe to be open and vulnerable, a place where individuals can be held accountable for their life in Christ, a place where they can truly grow in Him.

Not only must groups be open and the people in them mutually dependent on each other, they must also live in interdependence on other groups. Just as Christians do not exist in isolation, neither do small groups. Each group in the church lives in mutual dependence on other groups in the church, and the entire church lives in mutual dependence on all the other churches in the conference and in the world. All members of the entire Christian body are to live in mutual dependence on each other. Only when such mutual dependence is recognized and supported can a church really be the people of God living in community. In Christ there can be no independent Christians or independent small groups or independent churches. We are all to live our spiritual lives in mutual dependence on each other.

Therefore, Christian small groups should not be isolated even from other small groups. That is God's ideal plan for His church. These mutually dependent small groups not only minister to each other, but because of the interdependency of groups, they can also utilize the resources of other groups for members with special needs. If a person enters a group in a depressed state, the group might refer the individual to another group that can help with depression. All groups need each other. Above all else, however, for truly healthy group life to occur, there must be a spirit of openness and acceptance in the groups, so that the members can share their joys, their sorrows, their struggles, their failures, and their successes. God give us those kinds of groups in the church today.

Evangelism and Small Groups

This book has clearly established the fact that small groups were a vital part of the New Testament church. They are the natural place for member care to take place. However, little has been said about the advantage of small groups as an evangelizing agency. Before leaving the New Testament understanding of small groups, we wish to examine the part that small groups are to play in evangelism.

Before proceeding, it needs to be made clear that small groups are not the only way to do evangelism. For example, the New Testament clearly articulates public preaching of the Word to be one of the primary ways that the early church grew. However, the truly biblical church will make certain that all activities of the church have evangelism in mind. Therefore, biblical small groups must be evangelistic.

A caring community where members minister to each other is itself an evangelistic tool. Non-Christians seeing people living in a restored community, truly caring for each other, will flock to be a part of it. Such loving, caring communities are a drawing card for evangelism. People will beat a pathway to the door of churches that live in New Testament community. That may have been one of the reasons for the success of the early church. People today live in such broken communities that they will be anxious to be a part of a genuine, redemptive community. The tragedy of the church today is that it is more reflective of the broken communities of the world than of the restored communities Christ envisioned for His church. Yet it is precisely because the church has failed to teach its people genuine community living that the church has itself become a broken community in need of redemption. As the church once again begins to live in community, it will become an evangelistic agency. People cannot live in a genuine New Testament community and not be evangelistic.

Public evangelism and small groups thus are not mutually exclusive. Each needs the other. The public preaching of the Word must be reinforced by small groups or the preaching will not result in permanent converts. Likewise, the small group needs the public preaching of the Word to continually give it new converts to nurture and bring to new life in Christ. One of the tragedies of modern Adventism has been to make these two methodologies mutually exclusive. It is not a question of either/or. We need both public evangelism and small groups. Small groups will feed people to public evangelism for decisions for Christ, and public evangelism will feed people to small groups for follow up and discipleship.

Yet the small group itself must be a place of evangelistic activity. Small groups that only nurture themselves and fail to reach out to others will die. Navel-gazing groups are dysfunctional. When people belong to a small group, they are empowered by the Holy Spirit to reach out and touch other hurting people, bringing them into the restorative, redemptive atmosphere of their small group.

Discipleship always moves toward ministry and mission. In salvation history, God's people have been gathered for restoration and empowerment and sent out into mission. The small group is the gathering space to help people experience forgiveness, healing, encouragement, affirmation, trust, and courage. This is preparation to be sent back out into a hostile and alienated world that needs to hear, see, and touch the presence of Christ lived out through empowered individuals and groups. Jesus' early call to discipleship, "Follow me, and I will make you fishers of men [and women]," is an invitation to gather, to journey together, and to go out and minister to other hurting people. Every gathered group of disciples is in some way called to go out and fish, to seek others who also need the presence of Christ in their life.[2]

We have also seen that Jesus commanded the disciples to evangelize two by two, for ministry must occur in community. Individuals also need the support of the group as they evangelize. We cannot evangelize in isolation but only through group support. Only community can produce other communities.

The theological flaw is that these Christians meet together alone, and then go to witness alone. How wonderful it would be if they included each other in the relationship they establish with unbelievers and included unbelievers in their group life as well.[3]

The New Testament model indicates that disciples are best made in relationship with other disciples, which thereby indicates that ideally all new believers should be made a part of a small group and all small groups should consist of both believers and unbelievers. Involvement in the group must be seen as part of the evangelistic process. No longer must we evangelize in isolation, for disciples are made in relationships.

Adventist small groups have had a tendency to focus primarily on nurture. This is not healthy for the group. New Testament groups not only nurtured, but also reached out into the community and won people to Jesus Christ. The New Testament community group was an evangelistic group. People are best nurtured in the process of reaching others. Nurture cannot be separated from evangelism, nor can evangelism properly be separated from nurture. If we are going to pattern our small groups after the New Testament example, then these groups must also evangelize. This is an area that needs to be explored in greater depth in Adventism. We need to discover how to make our groups more evangelistic. Groups that focus only on nurture produce religious weaklings.[4] People are nurtured in groups as they go about fulfilling the commission of Jesus to make disciples of all people. This must be done in a community that supports the making of disciples and provides a "safe" place to bring the new or prospective disciple.

Summary of the New Testament Evidence

The New Testament reveals to us a restoration of God's original plan for humankind in the garden of Eden—a fellowship of people with God, mutually caring for each other. Jesus, by His redemptive activity, has restored fellowship with God; therefore, those who have been restored to the image of God now live in true fellowship with one another. We have discovered this concept to be a vital part of Jesus' ministry, as seen in His methodology of starting His church with a small group. It is further substantiated by the Holy Spirit at the Pentecost event by the establishment of house churches that became the norm for the New Testament period. One of the characteristics of such churches was that they continued in the apostles' fellowship. Paul gives us the theology behind this small group movement with his classic passages on community in Rom. 12 and 1 Cor. 12. The apostle John further declares this fellowship to be the very reason for the preaching of the Word or evangelization of unbelievers.

Thus, the New Testament has given us a theology and practice deeply rooted in community. The small group is the most logical place for the fulfillment of the kind of community demonstrated in the New Testament. The biblical evidence clearly points to the absolute necessity of small fellowship groups. These groups do not exist only to study the Bible but for the purpose of fellowship. The New Testament, therefore, demands that the church today have relational small groups, not as an option or as a program in the church, but as the very foundation of the church. It's time to return to the New Testament paradigm of church, which means a return to a small group model of church. If Adventists profess to be a biblical movement, we can no longer delay the implementation of the relational church as the norm for Christians. Let us return to our roots.

Notes:

1. 1 John 1:1-4, NASB.

2. Icenogle, 231.

3. Ralph W. Neighbour, Jr., *Where Do We Go From Here?*
    (Houston, TX: Touch, 1977), 61.

4. Ellen G. White, *Testimonies for the Church*, Vol. 7,
    (Mountain View, CA: Pacific Press, 1948), 18.

8

Apostasy and Restoration

The purpose of this chapter is to give a brief overview of small groups throughout the history of Christianity. Entire studies could be done in this area. Our purpose is to survey the demise of the small group church and the beginning of the institutional church. We also wish to look at the beginning of the restoration of the relational church in Methodism with its class meetings, which is one of the first Reformation attempts to recapture the early church model of church as community. Since Adventism has many roots in Methodism, this chapter will provide background material that will help us in our understanding of early Adventism, and especially Ellen White, as small groups were advocated in the pioneer days.

The Demise of the Small Group Church

At the end of the New Testament era, the church was built on community. Even as late as the end of the first century, the apostle John declared this to be the basis upon which the church was built. For the next two hundred years the church continued in the paradigm of house churches. During this period the church experienced substantial growth and seemingly was in good spiritual health, in spite of constant persecution.

The Christian church constructed no church buildings during this time. Believers continued to meet in homes, caves, or catacombs. The church was not centered in massive structures and buildings made of brick and mortar. It was built on the community life of the believers, who cared and supported each other as they continually extended their friendship to fellow sinners.

In the third century, Christians for the first time began building places for Christian gatherings. However, even these were very small. In viewing excavations of Palestinian towns, the author has observed the remains of third-century churches. They were no larger than most homes, and some small towns supported three or four of these small Christian churches. Evidently, when the church moved away from the home as the primary gathering place for Christians, the believers did not erect cathedrals. Instead their buildings were fashioned after the home. Of course, many Christians continued to meet in homes. These small, intricate fellowships were the foundation of life in the Christian community.

With the conversion of Constantine in the early fourth century, Christianity began to be tolerated and then became the only religion of the empire. This was the turning point in the establishment of the institutional church and the demise of the small group church. The paradigm shift that occurred in the fourth century has lasted fully seventeen centuries, and today we still suffer from the apostasies introduced by Constantine. The way we "do church" today is more a paradigm of the Roman Empire of the Middle Ages than of New Testament Christianity. We Adventists have been insistent that our theology be based on the New Testament, and we deplore the heresies introduced by Rome, yet we have unwittingly accepted Babylonian wine for our practice of church. We must not only come out of Babylon in doctrine, but also in practice. That clearly means a movement away from the institutional church and a return to the relational church.[1]

It was not more than three hundred years after this dramatic appearance of the apostolic small group movement in salvation history that the form and character of the church suddenly changed. The ecclesia as small group community disappeared and the church as formal institutional structure appeared. This transition was a major paradigm shift of the very nature of God's presence on earth.

It is generally affirmed today by theologians, historians, and ecclesiologists, that the church is at a dramatic "paradigm shift" in history. For the past seventeen hundred years, the realm of God has been strongly guided by this organizational and institutional mooring precipitated by the conversion of Constantine in A.D. 313.

> Instead of the congregation being a small group that constituted the church in that place, the understanding of the congregation had been enlarged to include everything in the Empire. The congregation was the church, the church was the Empire.[2]

Loren Mead continues to describe the church that developed in the Middle Ages. It was built on the assumption that the empire and the church were identical. To be born into the Empire was to be born into the church. Evangelism was the work of the soldiers, who conquered new territory for the Empire and subjected the people to Christianity. This resulted in a professional clergy, with the work of the church reserved for specialists. Large churches and cathedrals were erected, and the church adopted the model of the empire. Thus was born the institutional church.

The institutional church flourished throughout most of the Middle Ages and even into the Reformation period. Reformation churches merely copied the Roman pattern of "doing church." Membership in the churches of Luther and Zwingli was the same as citizenship in the state. Professional clergy administered the rites and ceremonies of the institutional church. The Anabaptists of the Reformation period developed the only church which was separate from the state.

They refused the protection of the state for fear that once the state was involved with the church, it would corrupt both the state and the church. The church they developed was persecuted. It had no safe place. As a result, the church took the form of a supporting community, meeting in homes and caves. Each community was small and provided real fellowship and support. Only thus was the church able to survive the heavy persecution inflicted upon it.

History teaches us that the only way the church has survived in times of persecution was for its members to be part of small relational groups that supported each other. As Adventists, we believe a time of persecution will come again in the last days. If we expect to survive in that critical time, we must begin now to develop small relational groups. If we don't create them now, how will we be able to do so in the difficult days ahead?

The Methodist Movement

John Wesley began his ministry in the eighteenth century. His preaching attracted large crowds of people who professed faith in Christ. Wesley was not alone in leading people to a renewed experience with Christ. One of his contemporaries was Jonathan Edwards, the fiery Calvinistic preacher who saw thousands come to faith in Christ under his preaching. Yet there was a major difference between Edwards and Wesley. Edwards would extend the invitation and then leave the converts, while Wesley would organize his converts into classes, or small groups. The result was that Wesley's fruit remained, while many of Edwards' converts reverted to the world.

The genius of Wesley was the small group movement that was attached to his preaching of the gospel. It is this that made Methodism unique in the churches that arose out of the Reformation. Thus an examination of the class meetings of early Methodism is essential to understanding the first real attempt to build a small group church by design in the Reformation period.

Wesley offered two types of small group experiences: the

classes and the bands. The bands were optional; the classes were required of all those who desired to stay in membership. The result was the establishment of an on-going system of pastoral care.

> Each group consisted of ten to twelve people from the same neighborhood, coming together weekly for an hour or so.[3]

> The leaders were lay people—some were men, but the majority were women—selected because of their high moral and spiritual character and common sense.[4]

It is interesting to note that most of the leaders of the early Methodist class meetings were women. This is especially enlightening when one realizes that the largest local church in the world today, Dr. Paul (David) Cho's church in Seoul, Korea, is built on small groups led primarily by women. Evidently women do a better job than men in relational small groups. Perhaps one of the problems in seeing small groups succeed in Adventism has been the fact that we have recruited more male leaders than female leaders.

What were those early Methodist class meetings like? In those early days, you could not belong to the Methodist church without being a member of the class and attending regularly. Failure to attend regularly was sufficient cause to be dropped from membership. Wesley believed in those class meetings so strongly that he made them a condition of membership. Today we would consider such a requirement to be oppressive. Yet we discover that this is precisely what the New Testament church did. Why? Because people could not be Christians if they failed to live in community with other Christians, and the small relational group was the ideal place for that community to occur.

In the early Methodist class meeting, the emphasis was not on doctrine but on discipleship.[5] The whole purpose of those meetings was to hold people accountable for their life in Christ. Wesley wisely understood the biblical principle that Christians will not grow in isolation from a community of

Christians who can hold them accountable. He formed these classes so that his converts could grow into spiritual maturity. The emphasis was clearly relational; the purpose was discipleship. These were not just small groups where people studied the Bible; their primary purpose was to build relationships. Bible study was used only to enhance relationships. These were not cognitive but relational meetings.

Wesley was convinced that only through an accountable fellowship could Christian discipleship be nurtured and made effective, and it is in such a context that the development of Methodist polity must be understood.[6]

> Wesleyan Methodism was a holiness movement and Wesley implanted a strong desire that Christians not merely accept Christ as Savior, but that they mature in their relationship to Him. Wesley perceived that spiritual growth takes place best in a group setting where there can be mutual support and encouragement for those pursuing the life of holiness. What was the content of such a meeting?

> Everyone was to speak "as freely, plainly and concisely as he [could] the real state of his heart, with his several temptations and deliverance, since the last time of meeting.[7]

> But at every meeting, there were five questions to be asked of everyone:
> What known Sin have you committed since our last Meeting?
> What Temptations have you met with?
> How were you delivered?
> What have you thought, said or done, of which you doubt whether it be a Sin or not?
> Have you nothing you desire to keep secret?[8]

Such openness would be unknown to most Christians today, even Methodists. Our American individualism would regard such questioning as an invasion of our privacy. Eighteenth-century Methodism did not regard it in that light. They saw such questioning as a means of helping people to be accountable. They questioned to hold people accountable, not to judge them.

Yet even the early Methodists recognized that this very direct questioning may have been a little too strong, so it was soon modified; however, the intent remained the same. The purpose of the class meeting was to hold people accountable for their life in Christ. This is perhaps one of the greatest needs of today's church, yet it scares us because the openness that it demands is totally foreign to our cultural setting today. However, if we truly desire to grow in Christ, we may need to drop our cultural American individualism and develop solid community once again so that we can truly experience life in Christ.

It was the optional bands that continued the more direct questioning of its members. The required class meeting did not have such direct questioning. Their initial purpose in meeting together each week was primarily to receive an offering. But community quickly developed in these meetings as well.

> It was therefore agreed that the members of each class should meet together once a week, not only to collect the weekly contributions, but also to give advice, reproof, or encouragement as needed. A dynamic of Christian fellowship quickly developed, as members began to "bear one another's burdens," and to "care for each other." The openness which was engendered by the meetings led to "a more endeared affection" between the members, and they felt free to be honest with each other.[9]

These class meetings very quickly developed a definite style of their own that encouraged people to be open and supportive of each other. Questions were asked, but they were not as specific as in the earlier meetings.

> After some such harangue as this, the leader proceeds to inquire into the state of every soul present, saying, "Well sister, or well brother, how do you

find the state of your soul this evening?" The member then proceeds, without rising, to unbosom his or her mind to the leader; not, as has often been said, by particular confession, but by a general recapitulation of what has passed in the mind during the week.[10]

Nonetheless, the point to be made is that the classes enjoyed this fellowship precisely because they did have the prior purpose of accountability. Initially there would be some awkwardness as the catechetical process was implemented, and people would be diffident about answering such direct and evaluative questions. But as the accountability was exercised, they began to realize that they were indeed on a common journey—and that their mutual accountability was not pejorative, but supportive. The fellowship was rich because they understood the real purpose of their gathering, and the meetings were informal because their structure was assured.[11]

Modern Christians would be frightened by such a meeting. This is because we have asked such questions for the sake of passing judgment on those thus questioned. We do not know the joy of mutual support and openness that the early Methodist enjoyed. Yet deep down, many modern Adventists still desire an experience that is reminiscent of life in the early Christian church. How wonderful it would be if we could eliminate our judgmentalism and the church could once again become a supporting environment. Small relational community support groups may well be part of the answer. Groups like Alcoholics Anonymous that practice such openness and direct questioning have been well received. If these groups can hold each other accountable, why is it so foreign to think that the church, which is called to be a redemptive community, can do the same?

The death of Wesley eventually led to the demise of the class meeting as a part of the Methodist experience. The nine-

teenth century saw the requirement become less demanding, until it was eventually eliminated as a condition of membership in 1889.[12] There was a bitter clash over the class
meeting and a compromise was finally reached. The class
meetings would continue, but failure to attend would no
longer be grounds for being dropped from membership in
the Methodist church.

The peculiar character of Methodism was thus changed
"from the condition of a society with some marks of a holi-
ness sect to the more conventional and less demanding character of a church."[13]

> . . . and in Wesley's day, they were primarily a
> means of "evangelism and conservation—the re-
> cruitment and assimilation of new members." The
> first half of the nineteenth century saw the loss of
> both of these functions. . . . References to class
> meetings in early Methodist autobiography decline
> quite abruptly during the 1830s, and the role they
> had hitherto served as a door into the societies was
> taken over by the prayer meeting—especially the
> after-preaching prayer meeting at the Communion
> rail or in the vestry. Indeed, spiritual vitality in gen-
> eral became more frequently related to prayer
> meetings than to classes. They were less structured
> and more spontaneous gatherings, and were more
> readily adaptable to the institutional activities of
> the chapel than the interpersonal spirituality of the
> class meeting.[14]

It is important to notice that as Adventism was beginning,
the Methodist class meeting was in the process of decline,
ultimately to be replaced by the prayer meeting. Yet the
Methodism that shaped the thinking of the early Adventist
pioneers, especially Ellen White, would have been the
Methodism of the class meeting, where there were definite
relational implications and accountability for their life in
Christ. In the next chapter we will examine the development
in early Adventism of similar methods of holding people accountable for their life in Christ. These were no doubt bor-

rowed from the Methodist heritage of such Adventist pioneers as Ellen White. While borrowed from her Methodist heritage, they became sanctioned by God for the Adventist church through the prophetic visions of Ellen White.

Watson concludes his penetrating analysis of the Methodist class meeting by declaring that the significance of the class meeting was not what it did for the Methodist church, but that it provided a safe place where people could be supported in their daily life and in their witness for Christ in the world.[15] He further indicates that the class meetings were not the primary focus of Wesley's evangelism—field preaching was. The class served the purpose of sustaining that which the field preaching had reached. It forced new converts into discipleship.[16]

Adventism, with its strong Methodist roots, has retained the field preaching, but has lost the small group that was also a vital part of Wesley's style. Without the small group component attached to our public evangelism, we stand to lose new converts, much as Whitfield did. The relational small group is part of the success formula of early Methodism, and likewise of early Adventism, as we shall see in the next chapter.

Thus early Methodism developed all the essentials of relational small groups that met together regularly for mutual support and encouragement and to hold each other accountable for their life in Christ. The Methodist class meeting had all the elements of small groups. This is the first time since the apostasy of Constantine and the establishment of the institutional church that a church which was built on relational small groups had gained such popular support. It must not be forgotten that much of Adventist understanding of church structure was borrowed from our Methodist roots. Even our conference organization is essentially Methodist in origin.

In the next chapter we will discover that another facet of Methodist practice, the class meeting, was also carried over into Adventism. However, it was renamed the "social meeting." It became the way by which early Adventists held each other accountable for their life in Christ. In examining early Methodism's class meetings, we have seen a return to a more biblical ecclesiology—the building of a church based more on community than on the development of large institutions. Early Adventism, on the other hand, attempted to build a church both as an institution and as a community at the same time. They seemingly succeeded, but institutionalism ultimately seems to have won out. Modern Adventism has resorted to a solely institutional church and has lost sight of the community-based church. It is for this reason that we reexamine early Adventism, which maintained so well the balance between institution and community. We must seek to revive this balance.

Notes:

1. The reader is urged not to confuse institutionalism with institutions. A relational church will have organization and institutions. Institutionalism refers instead to the understanding of church being the building, the organization, the program, etc., rather than the relationships between members. In the institutional church, it is the institution that must be preserved at all costs. Life centers around building up the institution. This is the Catholic medieval concept of church. This is the Babylonian wine that must be diminished.

2. Icenogle, 360-361 [includes quotation from Loren Mead, *The Once and Future Church*. (New York: Alban Institute, 1991), 15].

3. Mallison, 6.

4. Ibid. [Quoting James A. Davies, Article in *Christian Education Journal*, Vol. V, No. 2].

5. David Lowes Watson, *The Early Methodist Class Meeting* (Nashville: Discipleship Resources, 1987), 15.

6. Ibid., 67.

7. Ibid., 81.

8. Ibid., 84.

9. Ibid., 94.

10. Ibid., 96.

11. Ibid., 116.

12. Ibid., 137.

13. Ibid.

14. Ibid.

15. Ibid., 145.

16. Ibid., 149.

9

Adventism and the Social Meeting

S eventh-day Adventism arose in the mid-nineteenth century, just as the Methodist class meeting was being replaced by the prayer meeting. Formerly, all Methodists had been required to participate in the weekly class meeting held in a home, where people held each other accountable for their life in Christ. Now the prayer meeting, usually held after a regular preaching service at the church, emerged as the vehicle for accomplishing that.

It appears that the early Adventists, coming from Methodist roots, borrowed the idea of social meetings out of the Methodist prayer meeting as it was in transition from the class meetings. Most of the early Adventist social meetings were held after a preaching service and provided opportunity for people to share personally what the sermon said to them.

This concept was also utilized in connection with evangelistic meetings, as we shall see later. However, many times social meetings among members were held separately, rather than after a preaching service. So the Adventist model seems to be a combination of the class meetings and the early Methodist prayer meetings after preaching services.

Adventists seem to have borrowed the best of both worlds in the beginning—their social meetings seem to have been conducted in a manner similar to the prayer meetings of Methodism as they were in transition from the class meetings. While these meetings continued to decline in Methodism, they became a distinctive feature of early Adventism as it spread around the world.

Two sources of information exist about early Adventist social meetings: the writings of the early Adventist pioneers and the writings of Ellen G. White. In this chapter we will examine both of these sources to understand the early Adventist social meetings. Later we will draw some conclusions as to their function in the early Adventist church.

The Pioneers and the Social Meeting

As one peruses the early editions of the church paper, the *Advent Review and Sabbath Herald*, it is obvious that social meetings were considered a regular part of church life for most Adventists. In fact, these meetings seem to have been more important to the early believers than the preaching service. Preaching could be and frequently was omitted, but the social meeting was never to be neglected.

It is clear that these early social meetings were relational in nature. Little if any Bible study occurred there. The believers did not neglect group Bible study, but would follow it up with a social meeting where they could share together their life in Christ. This approach made the pioneers strong in both their understanding of the Bible and in their relationships with each other. Our modern method, however, has created people who are strong in neither Bible study nor relationships.

The social meeting took the form of testimonies, as believers shared with each other their struggles and victories in the Christian life and held each other accountable for their life in Christ. Uriah Smith, longtime early editor of the *Re-*

view, defined the early Adventist social meeting in this way:

A meeting characterized by spirited and soul-cheering testimonies, the beaming eye, the voice of praise, the earnest and stirring exhortation, and often the falling tear—scenes in which faith and love flame up anew.[1]

In the following quotations, one quickly catches the spirit of these early Adventist social meetings:

Social meetings were marked with great solemnity. Sins were confessed with tears, and there was a general breaking down before God, and strong pleadings for pardon, and a fitness to meet the Lord at his coming. And the humble disciples of the Lord did not seek his face in vain. Before that meeting closed, hundreds testified with tears of joy that they had sought the Lord and found him, and had tasted the sweets of sins forgiven.[2]

During one social meeting 117 testimonies were given in 53 minutes. All right to the point.[3]

If they ever have anything to say in social meeting, besides the ever-recurring formula, "I want to be a Christian, so that I may be saved," they tell only of a past experience, of the joy they had when they first believed. Of the joy of living for God, and of walking with him by faith, they know nothing, and he who tells of it speaks a strange language to them.[4]

In the evening following First-day we met for social meeting, and to break bread. There was a spirit of labor for the church, and some who had been bound in unbelief were set free and were filled with peace, joy, hope and faith. It was a glorious meeting.[5]

Prayer and social meetings upon the Sabbath should be sustained with spirit. A vigorous, holy energy that springs from the Christian's heart, should mark their progress. Here from week to week the consistent follower of the Lord delights to be found, punctually and faithfully at his post, cheerfully bearing his part, and from a rich fund of daily experience, he casts into the common stock his prayer of thanksgiving and supplication, word of exhortation, song of praise, all to the edifying of his brethren.[6]

These statements are typical of many describing what took place in the Adventist social meeting. It was clearly a time of sharing of one's life in Christ. Testimonies were freely offered. Sins were confessed and pardon freely granted. There seemed to be an openness in these meetings that hardly seems possible in today's individualized society. People openly shared their hopes and dreams, as well as their struggles. This common sharing, not of doctrinal truth but of Christian experience, was a vital part of early Adventism.

It appears that social meetings varied, but the common elements were prayer, testimony, words of encouragement to others, and song. The testimonies were short and to the point. However, at times some would resort to "preaching" as part of their testimony. This often provoked admonitions to keep the testimonies short and to the point. Thus in the quotation cited above, good social meetings consisted of many (117) testimonies in a short time (53 minutes). What made the meeting good was that the testimonies were short and to the point.

In all these descriptions of Adventist social meetings one element is missing: the mention of Bible study. With Adventism's heavy emphasis on Bible study, and the need of the pioneers to study and share the truths they had learned, this omission is astounding. It had to be deliberate, for they studied the Bible at other times. Obviously, the social meeting was not intended as the time for Bible study; it was totally relational. It included all the elements of what we today call small group activities, although the early Adventists used social meetings for both large and small groups. The point is that these meetings were held solely for relational purposes and to hold each other accountable for their life in Christ.

The social meeting was such a vital part of life for early Adventists that many times it was the only religious meeting that was attended. The early churches did not have regular pastors. All churches were taught to care for themselves; clergy were primarily church planters and evangelists, raising up new companies of believers. Only occasionally would a clergy person present a sermon. Most sermons to members occurred at the annual camp meeting, and even there they carried an evangelistic flavor.

This early Adventist model of church bears strong similarities to the early Christian church. Like early Christianity, Adventism was a church planting movement. All its resources were devoted to that purpose. Tithe was sent to the conference to sustain the preachers in raising up new churches. This is how Adventism developed a system whereby the pastor is paid by the conference rather than the local church. Since local churches did not have settled pastors, all the tithe was sent to sustain the church planters and evangelists, who were creating new work. Established churches felt no need of a pastor—they sustained their Christian life by themselves, just as the early Christians did. This was not an accidental development in Adventism but a deliberate strategy based on their study of the New Testament.[7]

How did the early Adventist believers sustain themselves in the faith without a settled pastor in their midst? Individually and collectively, they studied the Bible and read the Review. However, when they met together, they always had a social meeting. At times they had Sabbath School, but it was followed by the social meeting rather than a preaching service. It was primarily through the social meeting that the early Adventists sustained their religious life. In this way they created community among themselves. Listen to their voices:

> Here is an inspired delineation of certain Christian duties, duties which if properly discharged, will make us strong in the Lord and the power of his might. And one of them is faithfulness in the prayer

and social meeting. Then according to this injunction, as the church beholds the day of the Lord approaching they are to exhort each other in view of it.[8]

Dear Bro. White: Could you but realize the utter loneliness of some of the scattered brethren, situated far away from those of like faith, no one with whom they can converse upon the all-absorbing subject of their afflictions; no one with whom they can confidently unite their voice in prayer; no enjoyment of social meetings of those whose hearts unite and burn within them as they meet and sing and pray, and tell of their joys, their hopes, their trials, talk of our Great High Priest, of the new heavens and the new earth, and the sweet peace afforded them in obeying all the commandments of God.[9]

Evidently it was a great loss for some not to have fellowship with the believers. Clearly, the early Adventists were not isolationists in their Christian experience. This letter, printed in an early Review, reveals the great longing of an isolated member to have fellowship in social meetings with other believers. It was difficult to sustain spiritual life apart from the fellowship of the social meeting.

The need of these isolated members was not for a preacher to give them more biblical knowledge, not for someone to teach them the "truth." The great need of these believers was for fellowship with other believers. They knew they needed a relational meeting if they were going to grow spiritually. We read nothing here of being just as good a Christian without church fellowship— to them the opposite was true.

So strongly did the early Adventists feel about the social meeting that, as mentioned in the quotation cited above, it was considered a duty for the believers to attend the social meeting regularly. In fact, they felt that this was one of the first duties that Scripture had enjoined upon them. While attendance may not have been "required," it certainly was expected of every believer. People who deliberately absented themselves from social meetings were considered in need of spiritual help.

A couple of examples of life in the early Adventist church are revealed by letters sent to the Review by members describing life in their church on Sabbath:

> We meet every Sabbath for prayer and social meeting.[10]

> At the commencement of every Sabbath we meet together for prayer and exhortation, for which we receive a blessing. Sabbath morning is occupied in social meeting, Sabbath School, and Bible class.[11]

Thus, it seems that in the absence of resident clergy, the early Adventists sustained themselves through the social meeting, Sabbath School, and the Bible class. All of these, of course, are small group activities. The believers participated in these activities—they were not merely spectators. Social meetings, as we have seen, were definitely relational times. This in spite of the fact that early Adventists also spent much time studying their Bibles to discover truth. With such a strong emphasis on the cognitive, one would expect them to have neglected the relational, but they did not. The regular meetings of the church dealt more with the relational than the cognitive aspect.

A knowledge of truth without a sustained experience with God was anathema to early Adventists. That's why the social meeting was of such supreme importance to them. The truth which they had discovered had now been validated by a deeper experience with God. It was not merely truth for the sake of truth, but it was truth that led to a deeper relationship with God and with fellow believers, of which they testified freely in the social meetings.

When new churches were organized, the early church leaders seem to have been more concerned with the relational experience of believers than with their doctrinal purity. That seems amazing to modern Adventists, but is revealed very clearly by early church historian J. N. Loughborough. In the following statement, Loughborough defines the basis on which Adventist churches are to be organized:

> Where bodies of believers are brought out on the truth in new places, we would not recommend the immediate formation of a church. In such cases let a leader be appointed (this can perhaps best be done by the evangelist when he raises up the church), and let social meetings be continued till such time as the individuals become thoroughly acquainted with each other, and ascertain with whom they can have fellowship, and who are qualified for the important duties of officers of the church. As to the particular manner of organizing a church, when the proper time comes, we shall be allowed to avail ourselves of the experience of several ministers who have already adopted the following plan, and testify that it works well.[12]

This was evidently the plan of organization throughout the nineteenth century and even into the twentieth century. Here again we see social meetings as the primary means used by Adventist believers to maintain their regular religious services. Before a church was organized, it was important that the members know each other relationally, and the way to accomplish this in early Adventism, according to Loughborough, was to have social meetings.

What is so astounding here is that the leaders did not feel it essential that all the new members agreed to all the truths and continued to hold to them. Truth was important to these early Adventists, but equally important was the establishment of a relational church. If the believers could not get along with each other, even though they believed the "truth," they were not to be organized into a church. The creation of a new church implied that a relational church had been established. It seems that our pioneers were much more concerned with a relational church than we are today. Theirs was a New Testament faith, and such a faith demanded a relational church.

The practice of holding social meetings continued even after the organization of the church. These meetings were not just a part of the local church sustaining itself in the absence of a preacher. Early Adventists bemoaned the fact that the Battle Creek Church at denominational headquarters—the largest church in Adventism—was missing many blessings because they relied on preachers' sermons rather than on social meetings to sustain spiritual life:

> The church at Battle Creek needs these preachers less than any church in the State, from the fact that it has more active members than any other church in the State, many of them of long experience and sound judgment. We sometimes preach to them, but often feel when done that a social meeting would have been better. And it is frequently the case that, when we return from spending a Sabbath with some other church, we are told that the brethren enjoyed an excellent meeting, the best in several Sabbaths. Now what is the use for us preachers to get in the way of these experienced, living members?[13]

Can you imagine church members saying that they got along better without a preacher than with one? Even the preachers realized that they were in the way when they occupied the pulpits on Sabbath morning. Sabbath morning in early Adventist churches was not so much a time for preaching as it was for testimony and praise.

One can only wonder what would happen if churches today had an old-fashioned social meeting instead of preaching. Early Adventist clergy were needed for the establishment of new believers—the seasoned believers did not need to be preached at. The social meeting, with its testimonies, prayers, songs, and words of mutual encouragement was far better able to sustain their faith than the preaching of the denomination's best preachers at Battle Creek.

Not only were social meetings held at the local church level, but this practice was also a vital part of other Adventist gatherings, even the General Conference sessions. Examination of the General Conference Daily Schedules for the early days reveals that the social meetings were included as a part of the regular business and devotional agenda.[14] Even in those large gatherings the social meetings were a necessity. Believers needed to have time apart from business and theology to bond their life together in Christ. To facilitate more testimonies in these large gatherings, they divided the congregation into various groups, usually by ethnic origin.[15]

This brief examination of the pioneers and the social meeting reveals that social meetings were considered a vital necessity for early Adventists. They were the means by which the believers sustained their spiritual life in the absence of preachers in the local church. It seems clear from the evidence examined that early Adventists were as concerned for fellowship as they were for doctrine. While the distinctive doctrines were preached in an evangelistic setting, the converts were quickly taught to bond themselves together relationally by means of the social meetings. Early Adventists maintained a beautiful balance between the relational and the cognitive, while modern Adventists seem to be majoring in the cognitive and neglecting the relational. Perhaps it is time for modern Adventists to rediscover the balanced life of the cognitive and the relational. Perhaps it is time for fewer sermons and more fellowship. Small groups are an excellent venue for modern Adventists to rediscover their roots in the balance of the relational and cognitive ministries.

Ellen White and the Social Meeting

Perhaps no one has written more about the early Adventist social meeting than Ellen White. She not only participated in many of them, but gave much counsel on effectively conducting such meetings. The nearly three hundred references in her writings to the social meeting give us a fairly accurate picture of life in the early Adventist church as regards these meetings.

Ellen White confirms much of what other pioneer writers said about social meetings, but since her writing is more prolific, there are many more insights. In addition, Ellen White's prophetic vision gives her insights added power. To her, the social meeting was primarily a testimony meeting where brief testimonies were given about one's spiritual journey. Note the following excerpts from her writings describing the social meeting:

> We then had a social meeting. Many testimonies were borne and many confessions made well wet down with tears. It was a profitable meeting.[16]
>
> The five o'clock social meeting this morning was the best we have had. Brother was on his knees confessing to brother; there were broken hearts, tears, forgiveness, and rejoicing. We expect to see more of the salvation of God ere this meeting closes.[17]

From these experiences, it is evident that the social meetings consisted of more than testimonies. It was a time when confession was made, as well. People felt open enough to share their problems and confess the sins they had committed against other members of the church. It is quite evident that the Holy Spirit was the major motivator behind these confessions and that the setting of the social meeting allowed the Holy Spirit to be manifested in greater measure than in preaching services. Today we think of having an appeal at the end of the sermon. In those days the appeal was the social meeting, where all who desired had opportunity to share and respond as the Holy Spirit impressed their hearts.

Evidently early Adventism was able to engender a spirit of openness, where people felt free to share their problems and mistakes. Ellen White at times would publicly reveal people's wrongdoing that had been shown to her in vision. This was never done for the sake of passing judgment, as we so often do today, but for the sake of helping people deal with sin in their lives. Evidently, people felt safe, knowing that being open about sin in their lives helped keep them accountable and gain the victory God wanted for them.

The social meeting was of such importance to early Adventists that when Ellen White traveled to Europe in 1885-1887 and discovered that the Europeans had not been introduced to it, she immediately proceeded to initiate the practice:

I spoke in the forenoon, and then Elder Conradi said they had never had a social meeting. I told him now was the time to break them in. We had a very good social meeting. The meeting did not close until past one o'clock. It commenced at ten.[18]

Although the social meeting is a new thing, yet they are learning in the school of Christ and are overcoming fear and trembling. We keep before them the fact that the social meeting will be the best meeting in which they may be trained and educated to be witnesses for Christ.[19]

Ellen White considered the social meeting to be vital to the spiritual life of the church. She could not imagine the church without such meetings. The expansion of the churches in which she personally participated always included the conducting of the social meeting. But the social meeting consisted of more than confession—it was also a time when believers shared together their life in Christ, with its joys and sorrows. This was done for their own encouragement as well as the encouragement of others.

We had a good, profitable social meeting, then this afflicted sister spoke to me about her son they had buried a few weeks before, dying without hope, and the sorrow and grief she had felt.[20]

You can see from this text that the burden of the social meeting does not rest upon one individual, but upon all. We are to speak one to another.[21]

At every social meeting many testimonies were borne as to the peace, comfort, and joy the people had found in receiving light.[22]

In our next social meeting, nearly all who bore testimony expressed their thankfulness to God for the blessings which they had received the day before. Some stated that for the first time in their life they could say that they knew that their sins were forgiven. This was indeed a precious Sabbath to those assembled to worship God on this encampment.[23]

These descriptions indicate clearly that the social meeting was a time of sharing the joys and sorrows of life. It was a time when people felt open enough to share the details of their lives and testify to their hope in Christ. As a result of these meetings in which people shared so intimately, many left with the assurance of sins forgiven for the first time in their life.

Many times the social meeting was conducted at major Adventist events, such as camp meetings and General Conference sessions. It was perhaps at these events more than at the local church social meeting that Ellen White was a major participant. At the 1888 General Conference session, when the church struggled so intensely with the issue of righteousness by faith, many of the leaders had openly opposed Ellen White's ringing endorsement of salvation in Christ alone. The feelings ran deep, and the leaders were divided. It was in the social meeting at five thirty one morning when the tide began to turn in favor of a new experience with Christ. Listen as Ellen White describes the scene:

In the morning all nature seemed to be full of joyfulness. We assembled at half past five for social meeting. The spirit of the Lord was in our midst. Many stated that they came to the meeting with hearts as hard as stone, but as soon as they opened their lips to confess their faith in the love of Jesus, the light came in and their hearts were melted and subdued with the love of Jesus. One brother said he would bear his testimony for he knew it to be right, but he had no feeling. But his heart was broken, he fell upon the Rock and he was so impressed with the love of Jesus that he wept aloud. Ministers bore testimony that when they came to the meeting they were cold and their hearts hard, but when by faith they confessed to God their backsliding they knew Jesus forgave their sins and they were happy, newly converted, and they now bear a testimony that is free and joyful. "Thou shalt call his name Jesus, for he shall save his people from their sins."[24]

As I presented the goodness, the love, the tender compassion of our heavenly Father, I felt that the Spirit of the Lord was resting not only upon me but upon the people. Light and freedom and blessing came to the hearers and there was hearty response to the words spoken. The social meeting that followed evidenced that the Word had found lodgment in the hearts of the hearers. Many bore testimony that this day was the happiest of their lives, and it was indeed a precious season for we knew the presence of the Lord Jesus was in the assembly and that to bless. I knew that the special revealing of the Spirit of God was for a purpose, to quell the doubts, to roll back the tide of unbelief which had been admitted into hearts and minds concerning Sister White and the work the Lord had given her to do.[25]

The social meeting was what enabled the early Adventists to develop community among themselves. These relational meetings, where little Bible study occurred, afforded them the opportunity to share and confess, to encourage and to be encouraged. The social meeting appears to be the glue that held these early believers together. They could tolerate differences among themselves because they knew that they were fellow pilgrims in the journey. They could even honestly disagree on basic doctrines, such as the Trinity,[26] and yet the social meeting enabled them to stay in harmony. They were not afraid at times to admit that they were wrong. When they found themselves out of harmony with each other, it was usually through the social meeting that harmony was restored. The social meeting forced them to deal with differences with each other rather than to harbor those differences.

The social meetings were such a vital part of Adventism that Ellen White constantly counseled the church to make certain not to neglect these occasions of relational fellowship. In fact, she even went so far as to declare that a Christian is one who is active in social meetings, indicating thereby that one who is not attending social meeting is not a Christian.

> A Christian is a Christlike man, a Christlike woman, who is active in God's service, who is present at the social meeting, whose presence will encourage others also. Religion does not consist in works, but religion works; it is not dormant.[27]

> . . . and let every one who names the name of Christ have a testimony to bear in social meeting.[28]

Ellen White clearly felt that the social meeting was of utmost importance for the Christian. She knew nothing of an intellectualized Christianity that was all head knowledge. Ellen White's Christianity was a balance of mind and heart, of the cognitive and the relational. Throughout her ministry, and especially in the post-1888 years, we find that Ellen White constantly labored for believers to develop a relational experience with Christ. She did this primarily through social meetings. The only way to develop the relational life is to live in community with other Christians who will hold each other accountable for their spiritual growth. That is why Ellen White was so insistent that the church conduct regular social meetings. So important were these meetings, that, as we have seen, Ellen White indicated that people who did not involve themselves in these relational social meetings were not really Christians.

So vital were the social meetings to Ellen White that she often suggested it would be better for the church to leave off the preaching service and conduct only the social meeting. It was all right to have a social meeting without preaching, but it was not all right to have preaching without the social meeting.

> If fewer words of human wisdom, and more of the words of Christ, were spoken, if there were fewer sermons, and more social meetings, we

would find a different atmosphere pervade our churches and our camp meetings. Seasons of prayer should be held for the outpouring of the Holy Spirit.[29]

In addition, Ellen White counseled that conducting social meetings should be a part of the training of younger ministers:

> Our camp-meeting should be as a training school to our younger ministers. Here is the very place for them to be educated as to the best manner of labor. They should learn that all their duty is not comprised in preaching. They need to know how to conduct wisely the social meetings, how to teach the people to work, that there be no idlers in the vineyard of the Lord. While preaching is one of God's instrumentalities, there are other agencies that must be set in operation to prepare the way of the Lord. The church must be made to feel her accountability before the Lord will revive his work.[30]

Note that Ellen White connected the conducting of social meetings with the training of God's people to work for Him. The social meeting, with the requirement of sharing ones' life in Christ among the believers, was seen as an absolute necessity for developing the ability to work for the Master. One could not be expected to be involved in the work of God outside of the support of the community where that person shared his life in Christ. In Ellen White's mind, missionary activity arose out of the relational sharing that occurred in the social meeting:

> . . . and there had not been the habit of having social meetings in Europe. But we are seeking to educate them on this point, that it is the duty of everyone who loves God and the truth to speak to one another words of experience and of comfort, and to tell of God's goodness, His love, and His great mercy in giving His Son Jesus Christ to die for us while we were enemies to God.[31]

Here again Ellen White places the social meeting experience in the realm of duty. This performance of duty results in testimonies that cause us to share our faith with others so that they are reconciled to God. The understanding of the social meeting as duty reminds us again of the Methodist roots of this meeting and that John Wesley made it a requirement of membership to be involved in the class meeting. Ellen White seems to feel as strongly about the relational social meeting as Wesley felt about the relational class meeting. While she did not indicate that it should be a condition of membership, she clearly called it a duty.

Ellen White consistently labored against the notion that the local church needed the constant attention of the preacher in order to survive. In fact, she often counseled that just the opposite would occur if the church became preacher dependent. She felt that the church would become filled with "religious weaklings."[32] Life in the local church is to be maintained not by preaching services, but by the relational social meetings.

> Let every one consider the value of the social meetings, and let not large or small companies of believers think that they cannot have an enjoyable season unless they are entertained by a preacher. Where this dependence on the minister exists, the people fail to obtain that vigorous religious experience which they so much need wherever their lot may be cast. If the minister alone does all the witnessing, then those who have newly come to the faith become dwarfed and sickly for lack of opportunity to use their spiritual muscle. They have need to learn how to testify, how to pray, how to sing, to the glory of God: but failing to do this, they have only a one-sided experience.[33]

It is through the social meetings that the local church found spiritual health and energy, not by a preacher entertaining them each Sabbath. In fact, Ellen White clearly counseled that the church should not expect to have a sermon every Sabbath.[34] She also indicated that the social meetings were to be great seasons of joy, rejoicing, and praise. They were not gloomy sessions; happiness prevailed because of what Christ had done for them.

It is through the social meeting that the members attain the experience needed to feel free to testify for their faith in the world. Perhaps this is the reason so few Christians share their faith today. The loss of the social meeting has not only affected the quality of the relational life of the church, but it has also greatly affected the witnessing potential of the church in the larger community. As we discovered in our biblical study in an earlier chapter, the sharing of the faith always occurred in community. Early Adventism accomplished the same thing as the New Testament model in this area. It is time that we heed the counsel of Ellen White and restore a relational meeting to the church once again.

Ellen White has described these meetings for us. She has clearly counseled us on their absolute necessity, but she also includes much counsel on how to conduct these social meetings so that they do not become boring. She was vitally concerned that the social meeting be spiritually alive, as the people shared with one another. Testimonies offered were to be short and positive:

> The prayer and social meetings should be the most interesting gatherings that are held. Plans should be laid and wisdom sought of God, to conduct these meetings so that they will be interesting and attractive. The people hunger for the bread of life. If they find it at the prayer-meeting, they will go there to receive it. Long, prosy talks and prayers are out of place anywhere, and especially in the social meeting. They weary the angels as well as the people who listen to them. Our prayers should be short, and right to the point. Let the Spirit of God pervade the hearts of the worshipers, and it will sweep away all formality and dullness.[35]

> The prayer and social meetings should be a season of special help and encouragement. All should feel it a privilege to take part. Let every one who

bears the name of Christ have something to say in the social meeting. The testimonies should be short, and of a nature to help others. Nothing will so completely kill the spirit of devotion as for one person to take up twenty or thirty minutes in a long testimony. This means death to the spirituality of the meeting.[36]

The discourses should be short, and to the point, and followed by a spirited social meeting. Sometimes the social meeting would have the best influence to come first.[37]

As noted in some of these statements, Ellen White was very concerned about the character of the social meetings. They did not take place on the spur of the moment—they required preparation. The one in charge not only planned the social meeting but made certain that it did not get out of hand, with one person monopolizing the meeting or people giving dry, formalized testimonies. The social meeting was to be spiritually alive—it was not to be a time for complaining and sowing seeds of darkness:

We are not to bring complaints and murmuring into our testimony in the social meeting, but we are to talk of the blessed hope, to reflect as much light as possible upon the meeting. The Lord of heaven has represented himself as looking on with interest as the names and testimonies of those who fear and love him are written in his book of remembrance. Those who engage in this order of service, who speak often one to another, are to be gathered in the day when the Lord will make up his jewels; are to be spared as a man spareth his son that serveth him.[38]

In conducting large social meetings, Ellen White counseled that the congregation should be divided into smaller groups so that everyone would have an opportunity to speak. A leader was to be appointed over each of the groups.[39] She also counseled parents to help make the social meeting of high interest to children.[40] Even the lambs of the flock were to be a part of the community of faith in the social meeting. Finally, Ellen White was concerned that the prayers offered in the social meeting be short and to the point, and filled with spiritual life:

> In social meeting, prayer should be offered so that all may be edified; those who take part in this exercise should follow the example given in the Lord's beautiful prayer for the world. This prayer is simple, clear, comprehensive, and yet not long and spiritless, as the prayers offered in public sometimes are. These spiritless prayers might better not be uttered; for they are a mere form, without vital power, and they fail to bless or edify.[41]

Ellen White gives us another insight into the Adventist social meetings: they were a part of the evangelistic process. Today we would never think of using a testimony meeting as part of a public evangelistic event, yet Ellen White indicates that early Adventist evangelistic methodology did just that. People were not only brought into the church intellectually, they also were brought in relationally. Here again is the balance we so often note in Ellen White's counsel. The social meetings conducted during the evangelistic meetings were used to help people make decisions to follow Christ:

> After the discourse there was a social meeting and many testimonies borne, but I felt that souls were in peril. Souls were undecided and I urged that those who were not fully on the Lord's side should make decisions that day—should break the chains of the powers of Satan and be wholly the Lord's.[42]

> "These social meetings," she commented, "do more than preaching to ripen off the work."[43]

Ellen White also testifies that the social meetings were a regular part of Adventist corporate gatherings in the early years. As mentioned by other Adventist pioneers, the social meeting was the regular meeting of the church where there was no preacher available. And even if there was a preacher, there usually was a social meeting. This happened in both large and small churches.

> On the Sabbath the few friends here assembled in Edson's parlor for a Sabbath-school. There are four families—twelve persons in all—who usually meet for worship. Edson conducts the Sabbath-school when he is at home. After Sabbath-school they either have a Bible-reading or a prayer and social meeting. This is as it should be.[44]

Conclusions on Adventist Social Meetings

The early Adventist social meeting seems to have been very similar to the Methodist prayer meeting that was developing out of the class meeting at the time of Adventism's beginnings. Since Methodism was in transition at this time, we find remnants of both the class meeting and the prayer meeting in early Adventism. However, this prayer meeting is not to be confused with modern-day prayer meetings. It was the social meeting in Adventism. While Methodism was moving away from class meetings in homes to prayer meetings after a preaching service, Adventists continued both practices. They had social meetings after preaching, as well as social meetings in small home gatherings. These would have been more reminiscent of the Methodist class meetings, but not as structured with the pointed questions that Wesley asked.

It is safe to assume that the basic structure of the social meeting was borrowed from the Methodists, sanctioned by Ellen White, and then made a vital part of Adventist ecclesiology. Since the writings of Ellen White and a host of other pioneers refer to the social meeting, it must be assumed that the social meeting was not an isolated event. The regular mention of these meetings in the early Reviews would clearly indicate that they were a vital part of Adventist life.

The social meeting served to meet the relational needs of

the early Adventists. It was a time when people felt safe to share their problems and seek the help of others, knowing they would not be condemned, but helped. The openness so evident in these social meetings as believers openly shared seems strange to Adventist ears today, when most of us hide behind our masks. Certainly there was some hiding going on among these early Adventists, but there was definitely more openness than in the church today.

The social meeting was not a Bible study. It was a meeting where people simply shared what was happening in their personal and spiritual lives. Its purpose was not to convey knowledge, but to help members to share community. Its function was edification, not instruction. In a chapter entitled "Social Meetings," Ellen White clearly defines the purpose of these meetings as a place to share thoughts and feelings:

> What is the object of assembling together? Is it to inform God, to instruct Him by telling Him all we know in prayer? We meet together to edify one another by an interchange of thoughts and feelings, to gather strength, and light, and courage by becoming acquainted with one another's hopes and aspirations; and by our earnest, heartfelt prayers, offered up in faith, we receive refreshment and vigor from the Source of our strength. These meetings should be most precious seasons and should be made interesting to all who have any relish for religious things.[45]

Every indication from the writings of Ellen White is that the purpose of social meetings was to deal with the relational area of people's lives, including their feelings. She saw these meetings as absolutely essential for the life and health of the church. They were the means by which early Adventists maintained their faith. They did not have the disadvantage of listening to a preacher every Sabbath; therefore, they were forced to develop their own communal spiritual life, apart from clergy interference. The result was a very healthy, spiritual church.

When one examines early Adventist church life, it is evident that it was patterned, perhaps by accident rather than design, on the model of early New Testament worship. As we have seen, the early New Testament church was not dependent on regular preachers. Their church was a community based on fellowship rather than on doctrine alone. So was early Adventism. Certainly Ellen White had major influence in keeping the early Adventist church in harmony with the New Testament church's balance of the cognitive and the relational.

However, after the death of Ellen White in 1915, social meetings gradually faded and were replaced by the prayer meeting. Eventually Adventist churches began to pattern their services after those of other Protestant churches. Clergy eventually were appointed over the congregations. So the prayer meeting degenerated. Instead of a time for people to pray and share testimonies, it became another time for the pastor to preach or give a cognitive Bible study, followed by a season of prayer. The relational element was entirely lost in most churches. An unbalanced emphasis on the cognitive and eventually even a fear of the relational replaced the beautiful balance of early Adventism.

As a result, today many in the church consider it apostasy to have groups in the church that deal only with the relational area of life. A small group where people share their life in Christ together is looked upon as wrong by these people. They claim that people should only study the Bible in these groups and not deal with relationships. How far we have strayed! From a church with a beautiful, healthy balance between the cognitive and the relational, we have become a church where some members feel that such a meeting as the early Adventist social meeting is wrong.

It is time to recognize that such thinking is heretical, both to the New Testament and to our Adventist heritage. It is time to restore the relational meetings once again as a vital part of the Adventist weekly experience. The time has come for weekly relational small groups to be added to the Adventist calendar, and not only that, but once again to become a vital, dominant element in Adventist worship. Only thus can we be faithful to Scripture, to Ellen White, and to our Adventist heritage.

Notes:

1. Uriah Smith, *Advent Review and Sabbath Herald* (May 23, 1865).

2. James White, *Life Incidents*, vol. 1 (Battle Creek, MI: Steam Press of Seventh-day Adventist Publishing Association, 1868), 167. {Here James White is speaking of social meetings during the Millerite movement.)

3. J. N. Loughborough, *Miracles In My Life* (Reprinted by Leaves of Autumn books, Phoenix, AZ, 1987), 88.

4. E. J. Waggoner, "Living by Faith," *Signs of the Times*, 1889, 13.

5. James White, *Advent Review and Sabbath Herald*, vol. 4, no. 30 (Rochester, NY: May 29, 1855), 236.

6. F. W. Morse, *Advent Review and Sabbath Herald*, vol. 22, no. 15 (Battle Creek, MI: September 8, 1863), 114.

7. For further information on the clergy's role in the New Testament and early Adventism, see the author's work: *A Study of the Biblical Terms for Clergy and Their Historical Development in Christianity and Adventism.* It is available from NADEI, 9047-3 US 31 North, Berrien Springs, MI 49103, Telephone: (616) 471-9220.

8. G. W. A., *Advent Review and Sabbath Herald*, vol. 19, no. 3 (Battle Creek, MI: December 17, 1861), 20.

9. A. Chapman, *Advent Review and Sabbath Herald*, vol. 5 no. 11 (Rochester, NY: April 4, 1854), 87.

10. J. Hoffer, *Advent Review and Sabbath Herald*, vol.28, no. 6 (Battle Creek, MI: July 2, 1861).

11. Brother Holiday, *Advent Review and Sabbath Herald*, vol. 28, no. 5 (Battle Creek, MI: July 2, 1861).

12. J. H. Loughborough, *The Church: Its Organization, Order, and Discipline* (Mt. View, CA: Pacific Press, 1906), 126.

13. *Advent Review and Sabbath Herald*, vol. 20, no. 8 (July 22, 1862), 60.

14. *General Conference Bulletin*, 32nd Session (Lincoln, NE, Feb. 21, 1897,) 144. (This is only one example of many General Conference sessions.)

15. Ibid.

16. Ellen G. White, Manuscript 29 (1887), 267.

17. Ellen G. White, "The Southern California Camp Meeting," *Signs of the Times* (May 6, 1880).

18. Ellen G. White, *Manuscript Releases*, vol. 16, p. 251.

19. Ellen G. White, Manuscript 32 (1894), 3-5. (This is a reference to Ellen White introducing social meetings when she visited Australia in the 1890s.)

20. Ellen G. White, Manuscript 83 (Aug. 12, 1893), diary.

21. Ellen G. White, "Individual Responsibility in the Church," *Advent Review and Sabbath Herald* (October 22, 1889).

22. Ellen G. White, *Faith and Works* (Nashville, TN: Southern Publishing, 1979), 82.

23. Ellen G. White, "The Southern California Camp Meeting," *Signs of the Times* (May 6, 1880).

24. Ellen G. White, *The Ellen G. White 1888 Materials*, Vol. 1, (Washington, DC: The Ellen G. White Estate, 1987), 284.

25. Ellen G. White, "Looking Back at Minneapolis," *Manuscript Releases*, vol. 12, 183.

26. Uriah Smith, long time early editor of the Review, believed Christ to be a created being. While this belief was out of harmony with the main church, he was still accepted as a believer and given major church positions. This toleration of differences, the author believes, was due to the openness expressed in social meetings of early Adventists.

27. Ellen G. White, Letter 7, 1883 (quoted in *SDA Bible Commentary*, vol. 7, 935).

28. Ellen G. White, "Individual Responsibility in the Church," *Advent Review and Sabbath Herald* (Oct.22, 1889).

29. Ellen G. White, *Manuscript Releases*, vol. 2, 21.

30. Ellen G. White, "Labor at the Camp-Meetings," *Signs of the Times*, May 17, 1883.

31. Ellen G. White, *Manuscript Releases*, vol.9, 94.

32. Ellen G. White, *Testimonies for the Church*, Vol. 7, 58.

33. Ellen G. White, "Witnesses for Christ," *Advent Review and Sabbath Herald*, (Sept. 10, 1895).

34. Ellen G. White. *Evangelism*, 348.

35. Ellen G. White, "Christian Work," *Advent Review and Sabbath Herald*, (Oct. 10, 1882).

36. Ellen G. White, *Gospel Workers* (Washington, DC: Review and Herald Publishing Association, 1948), 171.

37. Ellen G. White, "Sanctification Through Obedience to the Truth," *Signs of the Times* (March 16, 1882).

38. Ellen G. White, "The Disciples of Christ Are One in Him," *Advent Review and Sabbath Herald* (November 12, 1889).

39. Ellen G. White, "Incidents of the Michigan Camp-Meeting," *Signs of the Times* (October 19, 1876).

40. Ellen G. White, "The New Heart," *Advent Review and Sabbath Herald* (April 14, 1885).

41. Ellen G. White, *Counsels to Parents, Teachers, and Students*, (Mountain View, CA: Pacific Press, 1943), 243.

42. D. A. Delafield, *Ellen G. White in Europe, 1885-1887* (Washington, DC: Review and Herald, 1975), 307 [quoting Ellen White].

43. Arthur White, *Ellen G. White*, Vol. 4: The Australian Years, 1891-1900 (Washington: Review and Herald, 1984), 104 [quoting Ellen White].

44. Ellen G. White, "Notes of Travel, Kansas City, Mo,": *Advent Review and Sabbath Herald*, (October 14, 1884).

45. Ellen G. White, *Testimonies for the Church*, Vol. 2, (Mountain View, CA: Pacific Press, 1948) 578.

10

Ellen White and Small Groups

The previous chapter has demonstrated that early Adventists were deeply concerned about maintaining a balance between the cognitive and the relational in their spiritual lives. The primary way in which they preserved the relational element was through the social meeting. The early Adventist social meeting was similar to our modern small group experience. Thus, the small group is one of the best ways to achieve the relational dynamic in our modern churches, provided these small groups are relational and not cognitive.

Some have suggested turning Sabbath School classes into small groups. However, if we make these relational, we will lose the cognitive element. This we cannot do—or we will become unbalanced in the opposite direction. What the church needs is balance between the cognitive and the relational. Therefore, we need two kinds of groups: relational small groups and Bible study groups.

In this chapter we wish to examine again the writings of Ellen White to ascertain if she gave any direct counsel on the formation of small groups. We need to discover if she advocated the use of small groups for evangelistic activity as well as for the nurture of believers. "Small group" is a fairly modern term that is used to describe the formation of a little gathering of people to nurture and care for each other, as well as to provide a safe place to invite unbelievers. Did Ellen White advocate such a use of small groups?

Ellen White rarely used the term "small group." Evidently it was not the "buzz" word in her day. However, she did talk about the concept. In doing so, she referred to them as "small companies," but, as will be seen, the meaning is the same. What did she have to say about these "small companies"? Her most emphatic statement is the following:

> The formation of small companies as a basis of Christian effort has been presented to me by One who cannot err. If there is a large number in the church, let the members be formed into small companies, to work not only for the church members, but for unbelievers. If in one place there are only two or three who know the truth, let them form themselves into a band of workers. Let them keep their bond of union unbroken, pressing together in love and unity, encouraging one another to advance, and gaining courage and strength from the assistance of the others. Let them reveal Christlike forbearance and patience, speaking no hasty words, using the talent of speech to build one another up in the most holy faith. Let them labor in Christlike love for those outside the fold, forgetting self in their endeavor to help others. As they work and pray in Christ's name, their numbers will increase, for the Saviour says: "If two of you shall agree on earth as touching anything that they shall ask, it shall be done for them of My Father which is in heaven." Matthew 18:19.[1]

You may search all the latest books on small groups, and you will not find a better definition of small groups than that given here by Ellen White. She declared that the idea of dividing the church into small companies was given to her by One who could not err. That is a divine authentication of small groups. Nothing could be clearer than this ringing endorsement which Ellen White gives to small group ministry. She then proceeds to define what should happen in small groups and indicates that they should concern themselves with evangelism, with prayer, with Bible study, with mutual encouragement and care, and that above all, they should build community.

This one statement should put to rest any misgivings that any Adventist might have about small group ministry. Ellen White could not have stated her case more clearly. The Adventist church is to be built on small group ministry. Anyone opposing this is out of harmony with both the Bible and Ellen White. We usually call this "heresy." Large churches should divide into small groups. If there are only two or three members in the church, they should still form a small group. The fact that Mrs. White advocates small groups for even two or three believers indicates that the purpose is not simply to create smaller units, but that the small group organization creates community.

When a church is built on small group ministry, it no longer needs a clergy person to be in control. As members care for themselves, the clergy are free to reach new people and raise up new churches. The small groups provide a basis for on-going nurture and care which is superior to clergy care. It would be impossible to return to the first century or early Adventist paradigm of not having settled pastors over churches without moving first to a small group model of church. Notice these thoughts from Ellen White:

> God's work is to be done in his way and his Spirit. In various places small companies are to consecrate themselves to God, body, soul, and spirit, and laying hold of the throne of God by faith they are to work zealously, keeping their souls in the love of God. The vital current of his love will make itself felt, and will be recognized as from heaven in the good works of his people. Those little companies who know the truth, with one voice should bid

their minister go to the lost sheep of the house of Israel. Each one should seek to do individual work for another. Not one who has tasted the goodness, the mercy, and the love of God, can be excused from working for the souls of others.[2]

As church members carried on their life in small groups, they would build a community that would keep them strong in the faith. They would not need a preacher to sustain their spiritual life, because that spiritual life would be strengthened in the community. Thus she invited them to beseech their pastor to go work for others. Note that the reason she gave as to why they did not need a settled pastor was the formation of the small companies, or groups.

The counsel to form the church into small groups was repeated in many of her books and articles,[3] which reveals that this was not a passing thought with her but a major concern. Each of these references repeats the thought that this idea was given to her by "One who could not err."

Ellen White also spoke favorably of the practice in our larger meetings of breaking the congregations into various small groups for prayer and mutual encouragement. She did not discourage large meetings. She enjoyed them, but she felt that something was missing if the small group element was not present as well.

> Sabbath there was deep feeling in the meeting; quite a number came forward for prayers, several who were making their first move on the Lord's side. After prayer was offered for these, they repaired in small companies to several tents, and a minister was chosen for each tent where they were gathered, and the work was carried forward that had begun in the large tent. These meetings were characterized by deep feeling.[4]

Ellen White also foresaw the day when, because of persecution, the large church would no longer exist, and the only way the church would be able to survive would be in small groups.[5] Christian history has proven that to be true in the past, and it has also held true in the present, as we have seen how the church survived communism. This was only possible through the small group house church.

Ellen White's strongest statements on small groups relate to their use as a basis for evangelism. Clearly, she did not advocate "solo" evangelism, but counseled that all such activity should be done under the support of a community. Therefore, it is not surprising that she talked so much about small companies as a basis for evangelistic work.

> In New York there should be several small companies established, and workers should be sent out. It does not follow that because a man is not ordained as a preacher he cannot work for God. Let such ones as these be taught how to work, then let them go out to labor. On returning, let them tell what they have done. Let them praise the Lord for His blessing, and then go out again. Encourage them. A few words of encouragement will be an inspiration to them.[6]

Note that Ellen White advocates small groups especially for large city work. The workers, whom she considers to be lay people as well as clergy, are to form small groups as the base from which they work. When they come back from their labor, they are to report to the community (small groups) that sent them out. She saw small groups as an excellent way to make certain that people did not get burned out in ministry but instead received the support needed to sustain them.

Not only were the groups to be a support base for ministry, but Ellen White also advocated that the small group itself become a ministering unit:

> Christ sought the people where they were and placed before them the great truths in regard to His kingdom. As He went from place to place, He blessed and comforted the suffering and healed the sick. This is our work. Small companies are to go forth to do the work to which Christ appointed

His disciples. While laboring as evangelists they can visit the sick, praying with them and, if need be, treating them, not with medicines but with the remedies provided in nature.[7]

Places that are unworked might have been entered, and souls might have been reached by the truth. Small companies of workers, under the wise generalship of consecrated teachers, should be going forth into needy fields. Whenever this work is taken up in earnest, careful movements will need to be made.[8]

Ellen White had a very balanced view of small groups, as seen from her major definition of small group ministry referred to in the beginning of this chapter. Hers was a very comprehensive understanding of small groups. It included not only evangelism, as we have seen, but also their meeting together for Bible study and prayer. Like the New Testament church, Ellen White saw that real church exists in community, with Bible study and prayer being conducted in small groups.

We will note first one of her statements on small groups as a basis for Bible study:

Let small companies assemble in the evening, at noon, or in the early morning to study the Bible. Let them have a season of prayer, that they may be strengthened, enlightened, and sanctified by the Holy Spirit. This work Christ wants to have done in the heart of every worker. If you yourselves will open the door to receive it, a great blessing will come to you. Angels of God will be in your assembly. You will feed upon the leaves of the tree of life. What testimonies you may bear of the loving acquaintance made with your fellow workers in these precious seasons when seeking the blessing of God. Let each tell his experience in simple words. This will bring more comfort and joy to the soul than all the pleasant instruments of music that could be brought into the churches. Christ will come into your hearts. It is by this means only that you can maintain your integrity.[9]

She envisioned these small companies meeting at different times in the day, rather than all at once. This is also advised by modern small group advocates. Furthermore, while Bible study is to occur in these groups, the above quotation makes clear that Bible study is only a small part of the activity of the group. There is also time for prayer, for testimonies, for sharing of life in Christ. In fact, the meeting described above sounds much like the social meetings discussed in the previous chapter. The point here is that Ellen White advocated that these things be done in small companies, not just in large meetings.

Ellen White talked in great depth on prayer in the small group setting. She felt that the small group was the natural place for people to pray together:

> Let the Los Angeles church have special seasons of prayer daily for the work that is being done. The blessing of the Lord will come to the church members who thus participate in the work, gathering in small groups daily to pray for its success. Thus the believers will obtain grace for themselves, and the work of the Lord will be advanced.[10]

> The Lord has promised that where two or three are met together in His name, there will He be in the midst. Those who meet together for prayer, will receive an unction from the Holy One. There is great need of secret prayer, but there is also need of several Christians meeting together, to unite with earnestness their petitions to God. In these small companies Jesus is present, and the love of souls is deepened in the heart, and the Spirit puts forth His mighty energies, that human agents may be exercised in regard to saving those who are lost.[11]

As a result of small groups praying together, Ellen White saw prayers being answered and the Holy Spirit being poured out. The end result of all this praying in small groups was the saving of souls. Small groups, for Ellen White, did not exist merely for the sake of having small groups. They were an instrumentality that brought Christians together for the reception of the Holy Spirit, which unleashed the power of heaven to win souls to Christ.

> Why do not believers feel a deeper, more earnest concern for those who are out of Christ? Why do not two or three meet together and plead with God for the salvation of some special one, and then for still another? In our churches let companies be formed for service. Let different ones unite in labor as fishers of men. Let them seek to gather souls from the corruption of the world into the saving purity of Christ's love.[12]

It is the church meeting together in small companies, pleading with God, that unleashes the power of Heaven. Believers are here counseled to pray for the salvation of lost persons and to solicit the small group to continually plead with Heaven for their salvation, until such ones come to faith in Christ. Ellen White personally demonstrated that in her young life. A group of her friends met together and prayed for their friends who were out of Christ until every one of them had yielded to Christ. She knew by experience the power of small groups in praying for lost people. The power of prayer in the small group cannot be underestimated. It is really the life of the small group. It is these prayers ascending to God through the centuries from believers meeting in small groups that God notices in the judgment:

> In the judgment many secret things will be revealed. Then we shall see what a belief in God's Word has done for men and women. It will be seen how small companies, sometimes not more than three or four, have gathered together in secret places to seek the Lord, and how they received light and grace, and rich gems of thought. The Holy Spirit was their teacher, and their lives revealed the bless-

ings that come from a possession of the oracles of
God.[13]

Ellen White not only advocated small groups in the church,
but also that they be used in the publishing work and in the
educational work of the church. No part of the work was to
be untouched by small group ministry:

> In the management of the schoolwork, small
> companies should be formed, who should be
> taught to carry a full sense of their responsibility.
> All these things cannot be accomplished at once,
> but we can begin to work in faith.[14]

> Cottages and buildings essential to the school-
> work are to be erected by the students themselves.
> These buildings should not be crowded close to-
> gether, or located near the school buildings proper.
> In the management of this work, small companies
> should be formed who should be taught to carry a
> full sense of their responsibility.[15]

> Let small companies [in our publishing houses]
> assemble together in the evening or early morning
> to study the Bible for themselves.[16]

Small groups were a comprehensive plan that should be
found in every branch of the work of the church. It is the
basis upon which ministry is to be conducted in the church,
in our schools, and even in the publishing work. To Ellen
White, small groups were not just a program of the church,
they were the major organizing principle of the work of the
church. To have a church without small groups operating in
it was anathema to Ellen White, for the church is to be built
on small groups.

In prophetic vision Ellen White saw a great revival taking
place in God's church at the end of time. When that revival
occurs, the church will once again assemble in small groups
to seek God:

> In the church there was a revival of the mission-
> ary spirit. An earnest desire to learn how to work

for the Lord was shown. Small companies gathered for prayer and Bible study. All moved forward with harmonious action. Believers went to places where the people have no opportunity to hear the Word of God and gathered the children for Sabbath School. Efforts were made to help isolated families. Plans were laid for these families to meet with other families for Bible study. Thus the way was opened for the light to shine forth from the word of God.[17]

Revival fires! How desperately the church of today needs such a revival. How then dare we resist entering into small group ministry? It is unthinkable for God's church at the close of human history to endeavor to carry on its ministry apart from a small group emphasis. One of the results of revival is meeting together in small groups to pray and encourage each other. There can be no genuine revival without such meetings. As we prepare for that revival, let's begin by meeting in small groups now.

Ellen White has given the Adventist church a ringing endorsement of small relational groups meeting together for prayer, Bible study, testimonies, mutual encouragement, and care. All of these small group experiences result in believers working for others in evangelism. To oppose a small group ministry in the Adventist church is to reject the counsel that God has given us through the inspired pen of Ellen White. It is time that the Seventh-day Adventist church restore the small group ministry to its proper place as the central organizing principle.

Notes:

1. Ellen G. White, *Testimonies for the Church,* vol 7 (Mountain View, CA: Pacific Press, 1948), 21,22.

2. Ellen G. White, "Followers of Christ Will be Missionaries,"

Advent Review and Sabbath Herald, (January 8, 1895).

3. The statement is repeated in the following books and articles: *Christian Service*, 72; *Evangelism*, 115; *Welfare Ministry*, 107; *Australasian Union Conference Record*, August 15, 1902; *Pacific Union Recorder*, October 9, 1902; *Advent Review and Sabbath Herald*, August 12, 1902.

4. Ellen G. White, "Sanctification," *Signs of the Times* (October 23, 1879).

5. Ellen G. White, *Manuscript Releases*, vol. 17, 350.

6. Ellen G. White, *Evangelism* (Washington, DC: Review and Herald, 1946), 389.

7. Ellen G. White, *Counsels on Health* (Mountain View, CA: Pacific Press, 1951). 501.

8. Ellen G. White, *Manuscript Releases*, vol. 21, 175.

9. Ellen G. White, *Testimonies*, vol. 7, 195.

10. Ellen G. White, *Evangelism* (Washington, DC: Review and Herald, 1946), 111.

11. Ellen G. White, *Lift Him Up* (Washington, DC: Review and Herald, 1988), 358.

12. Ellen G. White, *Testimonies*, Vol. 7, 21.

13. Ellen G. White, "They Shall Be Mine, Saith the Lord of Hosts," *Signs of the Times*, (November 23, 1904).

14. Ellen G. White, *Counsels to Parents, Teachers, and Students*, 311.

15. Ellen G. White, *Australasian Union Conference Record* (July 31, 1899), 6.

16. Ellen G. White. *Manuscript Releases*, vol. 9, 98.

17. Ellen White, "A Call to All Our People," *The Indiana Reporter*, February 25, 1903.

11

Return to the Biblical Model

Seventh-day Adventists profess to be a biblical movement, founded squarely on the Word of God as the basis for all our faith and practice. So states our first fundamental belief. How then can we, the Seventh-day Adventist Church, continue to exist as an institutional church rather than as a small group church? This book has examined extensively both the Old and New Testaments and has discovered that the biblical basis of all church organization is the small group. To be biblical, the church must be centered in small groups.

The church is not to be constructed like a corporation. It is not to be managed by one person at the top. It is to be divided into small groups where leadership is dispersed and lay people are empowered. The hierarchial structure that we have in the local church, with a pastor in charge, needs to move to a more "circular" plan of organization. The pastor will exist, but as an equal. Actually, many small congregations may not even need a pastor. Instead, as in the early Christian church and in the early Adventist church, the believers will be taught to maintain their spirituality without the help of clergy. The clergy will then be free to do the work commissioned for them by God, evangelizing and planting new churches.

Small Groups: The Center of Life for the Church

The biblical model we have examined does not indicate that we must add small groups as another program in the already crowded agenda of the church. Many churches have attempted to do this, and it has failed. When it is done in this way, small groups become popular for awhile but quickly die, because they are not seen as the organizing principle upon which the whole church is to be founded. Others have attempted to add small groups because it is the latest fad. However, two things should happen in a church before a small group ministry is begun.

First, a mission mentality should be rediscovered. As long as the church is looking inward, only nurture groups will develop. The church must rediscover a passion for lost people and feel a great desire to reach them. They must have a great burden for the many lost people in their community who are going to Christless graves, dying without hope.

Second, belief in the ministry of the laity must be restored. The church must rediscover the biblical truth that all believers are ministers and that the pastor is the trainer and equipper of the laity for their ministry. Every-member ministry must be seen as both in the church and in the world. The church must be committed to developing a lay ministry model of church where the pastor trains but the laity evangelize and care for each other.

Once these two concepts have been established, the church is ready for small group ministry. The two previous books in this series, *Revolution in the Church*, and *Radical Disciples for Revolutionary Churches* have dealt with these two areas. The point is raised here to make certain that these two concepts are clear before the church attempts to enter into the small group relational church model. Otherwise, small groups will end up as just another program added to the church. They quickly will diminish, life will return to normal, and it will be said, "Small groups don't work." If we are serious about returning to the mission-driven, lay-empowered, relational church centered in small group ministry, then it is imperative that we proceed correctly.

To be faithful to our biblical and historical heritage, we must completely restructure the local church so that small groups become the major organizing principle. Small groups cannot be optional, yet in most churches today they are considered so. Worship on Sabbath morning is considered "the event" that all believers should attend. In the church of the future, it must be seen that the small group is "the event" that all must attend each week. The worship service on Sabbath morning is more apt to be optional. That would be a more biblical model of church.

In other books, this author has suggested that the church of the future, to be biblical, must have a trained laity. Pastors must train their members for ministry, work themselves out of a job, and then go on to plant new churches. This biblical picture of the clergy is one that needs to be recaptured by the modern Adventist church. Ellen White long ago issued the call to the Adventist church:

> There should not be a call to have settled pastors over our churches, but let the life-giving power of the truth impress the individual members to act, leading them to labor interestedly to carry on efficient missionary work in each locality.[1]

In this new paradigm, how does the local church maintain itself without a settled pastor? By adopting the biblical pattern of small groups. That is what the New Testament church and the early Adventist church did. If it worked for them, it should work for us, even in the sophisticated twenty-first century.

What would the small group church look like? It would not be dependent on large buildings for its existence. In some areas, it might actually be a house church not connected organizationally to any church. It could be a church by itself. In larger areas, a local church might consist of many small groups. They might or might not have a building. They might rent a building for the times when they bring all the small groups together. The building is optional, because real ministry will occur not in the large meeting of the church but in the small groups. In this case, the church would be more like that of the early Adventists, who met regularly in small group social meetings and then occasionally, perhaps at camp meeting time, would come together as a larger group. In the church of the future, this coming together might not be as large as some of our modern camp meetings have become, but all the small groups in one particular city, whatever their number, might gather in one large group. This gathering might be weekly, monthly, or even quarterly. Large group life is not the crucial aspect of church—intimate small group ministry is where life is occurring.

In this biblical twenty-first century church, people would join the church through a small group. The small group would evangelize, nurture, and then support people in their ministry in the world for the Master. People would bring others to the small group to be nurtured as they were nurtured. Today people enter the church through the impersonal front door of the large worship service. As a result, they do not build relationships in the small group and enter into community.

The Structure of the Twenty-first-century Biblical Church

In the structure of this biblical twenty-first-century church, there would need to be a support base for the group leaders. This would necessitate ongoing training of existing and new small group leaders. This would be one of the responsibilities of clergy in this new paradigm. In a large area where there are many small groups, a resident clergy person would need to be involved in this ongoing training and oversight of the many small groups and be in charge at times when all the small groups would come together. The large gatherings could occur weekly, monthly, or quarterly. It would not matter, since the small group and not the large gathering is the lifeblood of the church.

In large areas with multiple small groups, the church might wish to develop a support structure similar to that which Moses developed under Jethro, where there were leaders of tens, fifties, hundreds, and thousands. The leader of ten in this model would be the small group leader, the leader of fifties would be a lay person who would supervise five small group leaders, the leader of hundreds would supervise ten small group leaders, and the leader of thousands would probably be the clergy person who would supervise and train the leaders of fifty and hundreds. Church growth expert Carl George provides excellent help for churches who wish to organize on the Jethro principle.[2]

However, the Jethro principle worked out by Carl George will only maintain an already existing structure of small groups. It will not enhance expansion and multiplication. If we are serious about the multiplication of groups, then George's structure will need some modification. In order for multiplication to occur, it may be necessary to have a leader who will coach no more than three small group leaders at one time. Ten is too many for multiplication to occur.

Second, in order for multiplication to occur, there must be careful selection of leaders. People who have not demonstrated in their lives that they know how to multiply should not be asked to lead. In other words, do not choose as small group leaders those who have not won at least one soul to Jesus. Such leaders will be unable to help their groups win souls. In addition, leaders whose small groups have not spawned at least one new group should never be chosen to lead out over three or ten small groups. Carrying this to its logical conclusion means that only people who have demonstrated their soul-winning abilities should be called to clergy positions, for only thus can we create churches who will reproduce and multiply, which is the desire of Jesus.

Another way to organize the church on the small group

model is offered by Ralph Neighbour,[3] and there may very well be others in addition to these. The purpose of this work is not to explore deeply these organizational plans. Others have done that adequately.[4] The purpose of this book is to lay out clearly the fact that this is the biblical paradigm for the church of the future. Each local church will need to decide how it will go about recreating the small group model, but the point is that it must make the small group the center of its organization. The life of the church must be centered in the small group.

Life in the Small Group

What happens in the biblical churches organized around small groups will be relational. They may, and should, study the Bible in these small groups, but relational issues will not be neglected. In fact, relational issues will be a major part of the life of small groups. In this sense they will be like the early Adventist social meetings. At that time, churches did not have regular preachers. Instead, believers met together for a Bible study in Sabbath School and then had a social meeting that was totally relational. Small groups in the biblical church of the future will likewise spend time in God's Word. Adventists can never neglect the study of the Bible. It is the foundation of our faith. We must never abandon Bible study in an attempt to become relational, but neither can we abandon the relational aspect in our attempt to be biblical. To do so would be unbiblical.

Let me suggest two scenarios for life in the small group church. The first is of a church that has its own building and continues to meet there every Sabbath. Members are encouraged to spend time studying the Word in Sabbath School classes that may consist of two or three small groups who meet together for a larger Sabbath School class. These groups might have multiplied from one original group, and the Sabbath School class provides a time when they can come back and fellowship together.

The groups then assemble in the sanctuary for Spirit-filled worship. Since they have been vitalized through the small group ministry, the worship service will be more praise-oriented, as the believers praise God for their spiritual life in Christ and with one another. Dry formalism is gone—vitality has replaced repetitive boredom. A sermon may be preached, but on many Sabbaths members of the various groups will share what is happening in their spiritual lives as a result of time spent in their small groups. Visitors usually will not attend the worship service for their first contact but will enter the church through the group. Thus, there usually would be few first-time visitors on Sabbath morning.

The life of this church really occurs in the small groups. Group membership in this church is not optional. As Ellen White indicated in the chapter on the social meeting, a Christian is one who is in attendance at the social meeting. If that is so, it is hard to imagine a person being a Christian and not being involved in a small group.

The small groups of this church meet during the week in members' homes. During the hour and a half to two hours that they spend together, the members share food in a get-acquainted time and talk about what has happened in their lives over the past week. People are open with each other. There is accountability. One member has previously mentioned that she has been struggling with anger at work, so at this meeting another member gently asks her how the struggle is going. A father has previously indicated that he has been frustrated in dealing with his teen-agers, and someone asks how they are doing. There is no thought of embarrassment or fear of judgment, but only a feeling of trust, knowing that fellow pilgrims in the small group are vitally interested in the members' spiritual development.

After sharing their life of the past week, the believers will spend time praying together for each other and for the salvation of lost people. These will not be perfunctory prayers, but earnest, heartfelt prayers that reveal the depths of their mutual experience in Christ. There may be some time for Bible study in the small group meeting, but if so, it will be of a relational nature rather than cognitive. Cognitive Bible study is reserved for Sabbath School. Here the emphasis is on what the Bible says to us personally. Here the believers apply the Bible to their daily lives.

Some have attempted to make Sabbath School combine both the relational and the cognitive. However, the early Adventist model separated the two and probably for good reasons. When both are attempted in Sabbath School or in the small group, it inevitably results in an overemphasis on the cognitive and the neglect of the relational. In order to prevent that, the early Adventist model should be followed, and there should be separate meetings for the knowledge of the Bible and the application of the Bible. That does not mean there is no Bible study in the relational meeting, but the emphasis is on application. Likewise, it does not mean that in Sabbath School there is no application. There must be. But the primary emphasis in Sabbath School will be the cognitive.

Sometime during this weekly small group relational meeting, there will be a discussion of the group's collective ministry. They may share what they are doing individually, but each small group will have a ministry that they share collectively. Perhaps the group conducts stress management classes as their ministry. Time is given to organize and plan for ministry.

Perhaps a member has brought a newcomer to the group for the first time. Time will be taken to develop a bond with this individual. As that person continues to come to the small group, a person with the gift of evangelism will arrange Bible studies to share the great truths of the Bible with him or her. The newcomer will also be invited to share in the group's experience on Sabbath morning. Eventually, hopefully, the person will accept Christ as Savior, be discipled by the group, and be baptized into the fellowship.

One of the temptations of moving into these new models is to neglect that which has worked in the past in Adventism. The early Adventist church, while operating as a relational small group church, nevertheless continued to reach people through the preaching of the Word. In fact, as mentioned earlier, the first-century church operated the same way. People were won through large preaching events and then placed in small groups. The small group church must be careful not to think that the only way to reach people is in the small group itself. Many will be won that way, but there are many others who can be won through large group preaching. Both approaches are biblical.

A church with many small groups may wish to sponsor a public evangelistic meeting or Prophecy Seminar. Those attending the groups who are ready would then be invited to this study of Adventism's rich prophetic teaching. When invitations are given to join the church, those who make decisions will be discipled much more easily in the small group where they have been attending already.

A small group church which neglects the public evangelistic reaping event probably will not grow rapidly. In attempting to copy other denominations who are moving into small group churches, we must remember that Adventism has a special message to teach people. This cannot be neglected. Many churches today are doing a fine job of bringing people to an initial faith in Christ. Adventism must do that, but it also must do more. It must bring people into full discipleship. Adventism's end-time message has been especially designed by God to bring people into full discipleship.[5] Evangelism in the small group church will utilize all means of bringing people to radical discipleship in Christ, including public evangelism. The difference in public evangelism in the small group church is that it will require little advertising because most of the people who attend will be coming from the small groups or relationships that members have been fostering in the world through their individual ministries.

This scenario has looked at group life as it could exist in a contemporary church which owns a building. It will take a massive reorganization of the church to accomplish this, but if we are serious about returning to a biblical model, this type of church will need to be created.

A Church Without a Building

In the second scenario we will look at a church that has no building large enough for all the believers to meet in at one time. In fact, this church is not even interested in having such a building, because the life of the church is bound up completely in the small groups rather than in maintaining expensive bricks and mortar. This church may be comprised of many small groups meeting in homes in the city—it just doesn't have a building. The groups may not meet together every Sabbath; they may come together for a combined worship experience only once a month or quarter.

Sabbath morning finds these groups gathering in various homes all over the city. They spend their time together studying the Bible in their home Sabbath School. Then they have a sharing time, similar to the social meeting of early Adventism,where they share their life in Christ. Children are not neglected—they are made a vital part of the group experience. The meeting usually ends with a fellowship meal where they break bread together as did the early disciples. There may at times be a communion service right there in the small group on Sabbath morning or at another time when they meet together.

In addition to the Sabbath morning small group, there would usually be at least one other small group meeting during the week. Here the activities would resemble those described in the first scenario, including their evangelistic activities. The difference between these two scenarios is what happens on Sabbath morning. In the first, the believers still assemble jointly in a church structure large enough to accommodate a large gathering. In the second, this meeting together of the multiple groups is not as necessary. Spiritual life is sustained almost exclusively in the group life. Only occasionally do all the groups come together.

The Pastor's Role

Both of the above scenarios would require a resident pastor in a large city who would be responsible to provide ongoing training for both current and new small group leaders. The pastor would meet regularly with the small group leaders to make certain that their groups remained spiritually healthy. He would also be responsible for the weekly, monthly, or quarterly combined worship service.

In the current institutional churches, the pastors spends most of their time just keeping the machinery rolling with all the programs the church operates. Considerable time is also spent ministering to the needs of the individual members. Since member care in the new model has been returned to its biblical base in the small group, much of the pastor's time should be freed up. This new time allotment must be used in two ways.

First, as we have already mentioned, the pastor must spend time with the group leaders. Second, the pastor should spend significant time starting new groups, an activity which would be similar to planting new churches. The focus of the new groups would be new believers. These new groups would be made by multiplying existing groups and forming new groups through evangelistic activity. Pastors in this model would be held accountable by the conference for the multiplication of their groups. Therefore, much of their time would be spent training leaders of the new groups of the ever-expanding church.

The pastor's key function then would be empowering the leaders and the formation of new groups. Rather than attempting to harness power, the pastor would be continually releasing power to the group leaders. Only as lay leaders are empowered can the church really become the church of Jesus Christ.

Isolated Groups

In this new paradigm there will be many places where there is only one group in a given city or town. In the old paradigm, it was difficult even to think of starting new work in these small places, because the church could not afford to pay a pastor to care for it. The current problem of multiple small churches that rarely grow, yet require the outlay of thousands of dollars to maintain, would be solved.

Many of these small churches are actually small groups already. Some smaller churches could be turned into two or three small groups. These groups could exist in the fashion of scenario two described above. There could be a pastor of all the isolated groups in a given conference; in some places that area might be the entire conference territory.

These churches would exist like the early Adventist churches without a settled pastor, maintaining themselves through their group life with regular "social meetings" (small groups). Perhaps on a quarterly, or even on a monthly basis, the pastor of this large district of isolated groups would bring all the groups together in a certain region to help the members feel they are part of a larger body. Again, however, the life of the church really would be in the small group.

In the present small church situation, a pastor may be placed over two, three, or four small rural churches with barely a hundred members between them. In the new scenario, the pastor may be responsible for what equals fifteen to twenty churches in the present model.

Yet the members would receive better care, as they followed the biblical model of caring for themselves, and their evangelistic potential would increase because the pastor would be free to start new groups. In that way it would be possible to have a "church" (defined as "a body of believers meeting together") in absolutely every small community in the world.

Is It Possible?

Perhaps this is just a "pipe dream." Can it be a reality? The kind of church we have described here seems far from the way we "do church" currently. Yet, as can be seen from this study, it is clearly the biblical model of the church as community. Not only does the New Testament advocate and practice this kind of church, but early Adventism also modeled this community-based, relationally built church.

Since the relational model of church is so strongly rooted in Scripture and in Adventist history, the present-day church of Jesus Christ should turn every stone necessary to return to the biblical model of church. The way may not be easy. In fact, it is apt to be quite difficult. Resistance will be great. Obstacles will be placed in the way. It may not be possible for all churches to move back into this biblical model—the resistance may be too great. Some will move faster than others. New churches will need to be started from scratch in this new model. But movement in the direction of reestablishing the relational Adventist church must begin, and begin now.

The Existing Church

Our traditional churches are caught in the life of the institutional church. They were organized in that fashion. It is the only life they have ever known. No members are left who remember Adventism from the days of the relational church. Our present church is primarily program based and departmentally structured, with youth, Sabbath School, Pathfinders, Community Service, Worship, etc. The new paradigm is a church where the small group is the organizing principle upon which everything in the church is based.

How do we transition from one to the other? Not by tearing down the old. The old is meaningful to a lot of people. They have been ministered to in the traditional institutional church throughout their entire spiritual life. They fail to see how the new model could be better. These people will give great resistance to a dismantling of the existing local church structure.

Jesus gave us some excellent counsel on transitioning from the old to the new when He talked about not putting new wine in old wineskins:

> No one tears a piece from a new garment and puts it on an old garment; otherwise he will both tear the new, and the piece from the new will not match the old. And no one puts new wine into old wineskins; otherwise the new wine will burst the skins, and it will be spilled out, and the skins will be ruined. But new wine must be put into fresh wineskins.[6]

Jesus' counsel is appropriate for us today. If we attempt to change the present church abruptly into the new paradigm, we run the risk of destroying both the new wine and the old wine. The transition has to occur slowly for existing churches. Traditional churches may never fully transition to the biblical model. Let them alone. Eventually, they will die, says Jesus. Instead, we must pour most of our energy into establishing new wineskins. Sometimes the new wineskin will need to be developed within the existing church. In other words, instead of eliminating the old way of doing things, add small groups alongside the existing situation. Eventually this "new wine" will take hold and become the whole, while the "old wine" slowly dies. But if we should seek to completely eliminate the old in order to create the new, Jesus indicates that we will destroy both.

Too many pastors have made the mistake of learning new ways of doing things and then rushing home to initiate them in their church. Quickly they discover that the members are not as enthusiastic about the change as the pastor is, and opposition mounts. The pastor becomes discouraged. The proposed new change is dropped, and the church sinks even lower into the doldrums of the institutional church.

How much better it is to disturb as little as possible the accustomed ways of doing things in the church. Introduce the new idea and let it exist side by side with the old. That is the only way to make the transition in an existing church. Even this may not work in some churches. In that case, just let the church continue with the old. Spend time creating entirely new wineskins. Some churches will move partially in this direction. That is fine. We are not on a time schedule. Give the Holy Spirit plenty of time to work. When God brought Israel out of Egypt, it took Him forty years to transition Israel out of Egyptian hierarchial thinking and establish them on the biblical model. And it took even longer for Egypt to get out of the people. We are not Moses, but we serve the same God as Moses did. Hopefully, it will not take us forty years. We trust this generation will not have to die in the wilderness. God today needs leaders who will be the new

Moses to lead His people out of Egypt and into the prom-
ised land. It's time to start leading the church back to the
biblical pattern. God calls for such leaders now.

Pastors who are able only to partially transition the church
during their time of ministry can be thankful that at least
God has enabled them to move in the right direction. The
most important priority for the existing church is to restore
relational meetings, even though it may never totally develop
the small group model. In some churches these relational
meetings may not even be in the form of a small group. Relational times can be introduced in the large group events as
well. However, the relational issue cannot be optional for us
as a biblical church. The way we accomplish relational ministry may be optional, but the church must become relational
or it will cease to be the church of Jesus Christ.

The easiest route to the new paradigm is to establish new
churches which from the beginning are organized on the
small group model. Here one does not have to overcome
the tradition of the existing church, but from its inception
the members can be educated in the biblical model of the
small group church. As these models of the new paradigm
begin to grow and prosper under the blessing of the Holy
Spirit, existing churches will be encouraged to copy their
model. And prosper they will, for God will bless His church
as it seeks to return to a biblical model of "doing church."

This biblical model of the church is being rediscovered
today not just in Adventist churches but in countless churches
around the world. It will be the church of the future. God is
raising up people all over the world to lead the church to
the new paradigm. Carl George has indicated that this will
be a key characteristic of the churches that survive into the
twenty-first century. Most of the others will die.

> In a nutshell, what is the fundamental active in-
> gredient in the church of the future? Growing cells
> led by volunteer ministers are the fundamental
> building block. Everything else can be rationalized
> around that one concept.[7]

The apostle John stated it so clearly at the end of the first century when he declared that we preach this message of cognitive truth so that people might have fellowship with us, as we have fellowship with the Father and His Son.[8] The basic need of humanity has not changed in two thousand years. God is still calling out a people who will live in true community and thus demonstrate to the world the transforming nature of the community God has called into being. Christians can no longer live in isolation—they are called to live in community:

> To learn to trust, and to become trustworthy— to learn to love, and to become loving—we must become deeply involved in the lives of others, to whom we commit ourselves in Christ. To develop this kind of relationship, we need to share ourselves with others, and they need to share themselves with us. All of this demands time. More than this, it requires a face-to-face relationship. A relationship we can have only with a few others at one time. And thus a church is forced to move to a small group structure.[9]

> We are called to live out our Christian life in community.[10]

This is the call of God at the end of the twentieth century. We have followed the pattern of the institutional church, organized by Constantine in the fourth century, long enough. It doesn't work. It is time to create a church built on biblical foundations. The Adventist church has constructed what we believe to be a clear platform of biblical truth, but we must now create also a clear platform of biblical practice. It is not sufficient to simply believe the truths of the Bible. Those truths must be lived out by those who believe. Adventists began in the biblical model; it is now time to return to our roots.

Not only must these truths be lived out in our lives, but God has called us also to live our lives in community with others. Sadly, we have built our church on American individualism rather than on biblical community. It is time to forsake our individualism in favor of establishing biblical community. Let's begin now!

Notes:

1. Ellen G. White, "The Work in Greater New York," *Atlantic Union Gleaner,* (January 8, 1902).

2. Carl George, *Prepare Your Church for the Future* (Grand Rapids: Fleming H. Revell, 1992) and *The Coming Church Revolution* (Grand Rapids: Fleming H. Revell, 1994).

3. Ralph W. Neighbour, Jr., *Where Do We Go From Here?* (Houston, TX: Touch Publications, 1990).

4. At the date of this writing, other Adventist authors are working on a model of what a cell church would look like. Look for publications in this area in the near future.

5. See my book, *Radical Disciples For Revolutionary Churches*, (Hart Research Center: Fallbrook, CA: 1996).

6. Luke 5:36-38, NASB.

7. George, *The Coming Church Revolution,* 313.

8. 1 John 1:1-5.

9. Mallison, 9 [quoting Lawrence Richards].

10. Ibid.